# Country Quilt Patterns

Mary Elizabeth Johnson

Oxmoor House, Inc., Birmingham

Copyright © 1977 by Oxmoor House, Inc.
Book Division of The Progressive Farmer Company
P.O. Box 2463, Birmingham, Alabama 35202

Library of Congress Catalog Card Number: 77–75689
ISBN: 0–8487–0478–9
Manufactured in the United States of America
First Printing 1977

*Country Quilt Patterns*

Photography: David Matthews, Steve Logan
Line drawings in pattern section: June Taylor Shrum


The author wishes to give special thanks to those who
made photographing the full-size quilts possible:

Mrs. Clifford Westerfield, Sara Jane Ball, Mrs. Mamie
Heasley, Mrs. Hugh Puckett, and Mrs. Dorothy
Burnette.

*This truly exquisite quilt was created by Mrs. Clifford Westerfield of Athens, Georgia. The name of the pattern is Cherokee Rose, and although the overall design resembles the rambling wildflower for which it is named, the quilt is actually made up of identical blocks set side by side. All leaves and flowers are padded and stitched onto the background, then outlined with embroidery stitches and quilting. Flower stems and centers are created with a variety of embroidery stitches. Mrs. Westerfield's delicately beautiful color scheme is particularly effective and is accented by reversing the placement of the blue and white for the scalloped border. The sophistication of the quilting pattern in the open areas of the quilt is another feature that makes this quilt a masterpiece.* Pattern begins on page 25.

# The Designs

One of the nicest things about quilting is that it is an art form that is carried on out of love. Mrs. Heasley, shown at left at work on her *Calico Bouquet* quilt, has always found time to quilt even though she was busy keeping house, having a family, and contributing to a working farm. She has a treasure trove of lovely quilts that she has stitched herself. And because she has always quilted simply out of love of the craft, no one was more surprised than she when one of her quilts was chosen for the cover of this book!

Presented in this book are 23 sparkling and original quilt designs. They are the handiwork of the women whose names appear with each quilt pattern. The designs were submitted to *Progressive Farmer* magazine's Country Living Quilt Block Contest, which drew hundreds of entries. Each design was based on some aspect of rural heritage. For many of the women who entered the contest, the inspiration for their designs could be seen right outside the kitchen window; for others, the inspiration was a treasured memory of another time when they actually lived in the country. Tales and Indian lore jogged the thought processes of many entrants. Patriotic themes and ideals stirred others. These quilt blocks are an outpouring of creative energy that is astonishing—representing a heritage of generations of American folk artists.

We want you to enjoy using the patterns in this book, and at the same time, we'd like to think they will encourage you to create your own quilt patterns. There is nothing so rewarding as creating something that is truly from your own experience and interest. Although you perform a creative process each time you choose colors and fabrics for any quilt design, it is even more fulfilling to work out the entire design. The women whose work is represented in this book are united by a common motive: they love to quilt. They are not so very different from any of you. Read the stories that accompany each quilt pattern to see what inspired each woman to create her own special design.

Browse through the following pages and let the color photographs of the quilt designs inspire you and set your fingers flying. If you are a new quilter, welcome to one of the most satisfying pastimes you will ever enjoy. If you are an old hand, help yourself to the inspiration and new challenges represented by this collection of enchanting designs.

*Mrs. Mamie Heasley of Little Rock, Arkansas, is shown quilting another block of her* Calico Bouquet *pattern. She has made the entire quilt using the apartment quilting technique, adding blocks to the quilt when she has enough to make one row. Her quilt, which is also featured on our cover, is a wonderful patchwork design of Mrs. Heasley's own devising. The solid green blocks with their diagonal quilting play a fine counterpoint to the gaily patterned calico bouquets. Pattern begins on page 22.*

*Note:* Guidelines for designing your own quilt block, plus detailed instructions on how to make quilts, including hand and machine techniques for appliqué, patchwork, embroidery, trapunto, and so on, plus fifty other different and original designs may be found in *Prize Country Quilts* by Mary Elizabeth Johnson, Oxmoor House, © 1977. Information about ordering this 240-page hardbound book can be obtained by writing the publisher at    P.O. Box 2463, Birmingham, Alabama 35202.

*Amelia's Gemstone,* p. 16

*Bicentennial Star,* p. 18

*Birds and Flowers,* p. 20

*Calico Bouquet,* p. 22

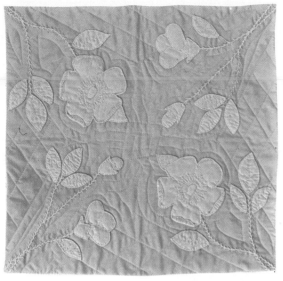

*Cherokee Rose*, p. 25

*Donkey*, p. 28

*Evergreens*, p. 30

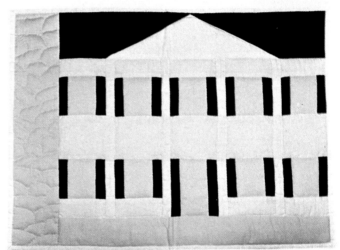

*Fields' Lost Acre*, p. 32

*God's Bounty, p. 36*

*Great Grandma, p. 39*

*Green It Up Again, p. 43*

*Log Schoolhouse, p. 47*

*Magnolia Blossom*, p. 49

*My Grandmother's Rose*, p. 53

*No Name*, p. 55

*Pioneer Apple*, p. 57

*South's Pride Daisy*, p. 60

*Sweetheart*, p. 63

*Tiny Stars and Squares*, p. 65

*Tractor Pull*, p. 67

10

*Tranquility, p. 70*

*USA, p. 77*

*Wheel, p. 79*

# The Patterns

The remainder of this book is devoted to the patterns for the designs shown on pages 6 through 11. All patterns have been tested for accuracy, and quilt blocks have been made from each pattern in firmly woven fabric. Keep in mind that different fabrics and different people will cause quilt patterns to work up differently. Test any pattern you plan to make in the fabric you plan to use to make sure the pattern works for you before you begin a major project with it.

The color photographs of the quilt designs are arranged alphabetically, as are the patterns in the following section. Each pattern is accompanied by a story from the designer. Keep in mind as you work with these quilt patterns that you can and should change the color schemes to suit your own personal preferences.

## GUIDE TO USING THE PATTERNS

- Use the printed patterns in this book as a guide to make your own patterns rather than cut apart these pages. Trace our patterns onto your own paper, taking note of any special instructions printed on the pieces or in the accompanying text. Then make templates from your patterns to use in cutting your fabric pieces.
- Wherever possible, the pattern pieces in this book are drawn to actual size. Exceptions are noted on individual pieces by either a fold line or a jagged line and instructions in the text for enlarging to proper size.
- All pattern pieces include a seam allowance of ¼" (6mm) except in special cases. Exceptions are noted on individual pieces.
- The number and type of pattern pieces needed for one quilt block are listed in the text accompanying each pattern.
- Quilting patterns are included for each block. The quilting patterns do not attempt to show size of stitches, only where the stitches should be placed. In outline quilting, the quilting stitches are placed ¼" (6mm) from the finished edge of the shape being outlined.
- If a quilt block is made of one small unit repeated many times, only the single unit is shown in the piecing and quilting diagrams in most cases. (The most common example of this is when the quilt block is made of four identical quarters.) When this integral unit is quite small, the entire quilt block, rather than just the single unit, is shown.
- If a pattern requires that a piece be cut for right and left sides, be certain to cut one side with the pattern piece right side up and the other side with the pattern piece wrong side up.

The following page contains the key to the pattern symbols. Be sure to study the key before you begin working with the patterns and refer to the key if there is something you do not understand.

---

*A traditional quilt form is the album quilt. This one, designed and stitched by Mrs. Velma Culbert, has become a treasured family heirloom. It depicts the great-grandmother attending to the various chores that were necessary on a working farm. The sunbonneted lady is seen feeding the chickens, tending to her flower garden, and gathering pumpkins and watermelons. These squares are alternated with contrasting squares that represent other memories precious to the family. You may wish to follow Mrs. Culbert's suggestions for interpreting other activities of the great-grandmother, or better yet, you may draw upon your own family memories to create a truly personal quilt. The pattern for one block of the* Great Grandma *quilt begins on page 39.*

# KEY TO PATTERN SYMBOLS

———————————————————————————— Cutting line

— — — — — — — — Stitching line

◄——————————————————————► Grain line (preferred direction for placement of pattern piece on fabric)

– – – – – – – – – – – – – – Gathering line (guide for placement of ease stitching)

•••••••••••••••••••••••••••••• Embroidery stitch placement

A section of the pattern has been omitted. Read the cutting instructions in the text.

Place on the fold. This indicates that only half of the pattern is given; the line on which this bracket appears must be placed on the fold *when making your pattern, not when cutting your fabric.* The place-on-the-fold-line edge becomes the center line of your pattern piece.

The last page of pattern pieces for this particular design. Be sure to turn the pages until you see this symbol to make sure you have seen all the pieces for your chosen design.

---

*The presentation quilt is another traditional quilt form, and* Amelia's Gemstone *is as fine an example as you will find anywhere. Designed by Mrs. Dorothy Burnette as a commemorative banner for the Virginia county for which it is named, the quilt now hangs on public display in the local museum. It was stitched by a member of the Amelia County Home Demonstration Club as a special Bicentennial keep-sake to be added to the county's historical treasures. Most often, presentation quilts are intended primarily as show-pieces of fine design and top-quality workmanship rather than as utilitarian bedcoverings. The 200th birthday of the United States inspired many groups around the country to create keepsakes such as this. Pattern begins on page 16.*

# AMELIA'S GEMSTONE
Mrs. Dorothy T. Burnette
Amelia, Virginia

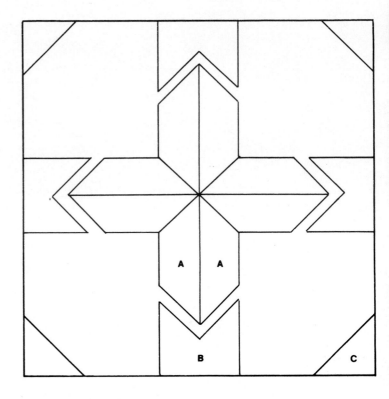

"The desire for a permanent keep-sake led the Amelia County Extension Homemaker's Clubs to ask me to design a quilt that would become part of the county's historical treasure. Interest in quilts, old and new, runs high among our homemakers. Several members have set high standards for fine quilting.

"Amelia is a rural county, with homemakers living close to the land. Roots run deep. The county boasts a large variety of minerals—gems and gemstones. Consequently, rock hounds ply their trade here year round. Most families have at least a few of these bits of rock keepsakes. From these, the *Amelia's Gemstone* idea originated.

"The angles and colors characteristic of many gems and gemstones in the county were influential in my design. Blues and reds seemed most predominant—the blues of the bluish-green amazonstone, the pale blue iridescence of the moonstones, the reddish-orange-brown colors of the spessartite (a variety of garnet), and the beautiful red to yellow of the microlite."

One of the interesting things about this quilt block is that it looks like patchwork, but it is actually appliqué. Quilt blocks should be set directly next to one another so that the secondary crosses can be formed. A border of the same fabric as the secondary crosses is a nice finishing touch, as shown on the preceding page.

Each finished block measures 13½" (34.3cm) square.

One block takes the following:
A—8 sections for center cross
B—4 sections for secondary cross
C—4 corner triangles
Background square—14" x 14" (35.6cm x 35.6cm)

Carefully mark the placement of the quilting stitching after the design has been appliquéd in place.

16

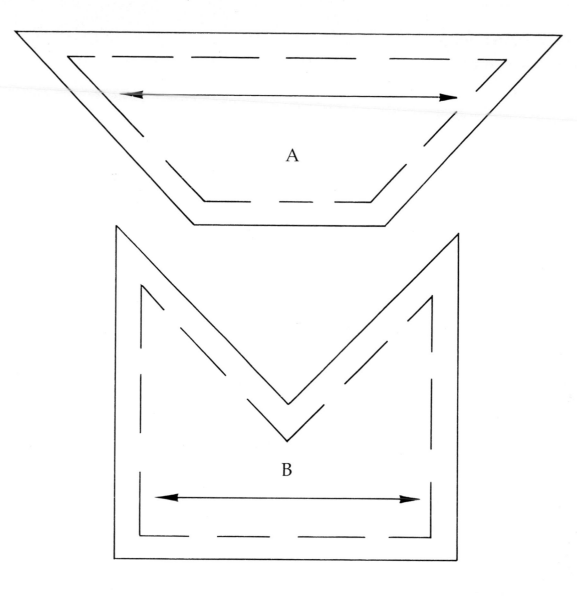

A

B

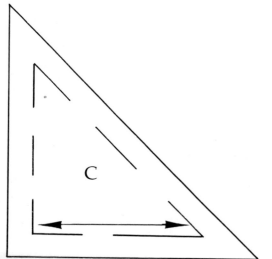

C

# BICENTENNIAL STAR
Mrs. Clarence Scruggs
Fairfield, Texas

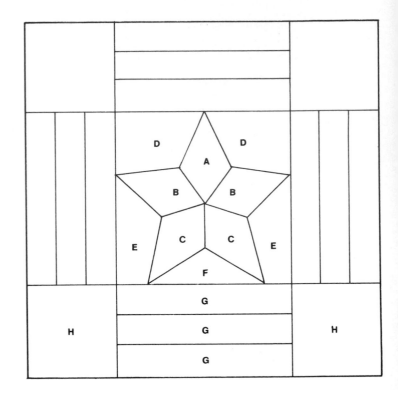

"The inspiration for this design was taken from an American Bicentennial tray. To celebrate the 1976 Bicentennial year, I wanted to make each of my two sons a five-pointed star quilt. One son and I figured out a design for a small star; by measuring the angles with a protractor, I finally got the star the right size—the rest was easy. Then, after all that work, I saw directions in a child's book for folding paper to make a star!"

Mrs. Scruggs' original design is a bright, patriotic piece of folk art. You will notice that the center star is made of diamonds of three different sizes. The colors of the American flag are balanced in just the right proportions for a crisp effect. Navy blue sashing could be used between blocks.

Each finished block measures 13½" (34.3cm) square.

One block takes the following:
A— 1 white star point
B— 2 white side star points
C— 2 white bottom star points
D— 2 navy top backgrounds
E— 2 navy side backgrounds
F— 1 navy bottom background

G—12 total:
    8 red
    4 white
H— 4 navy corner squares

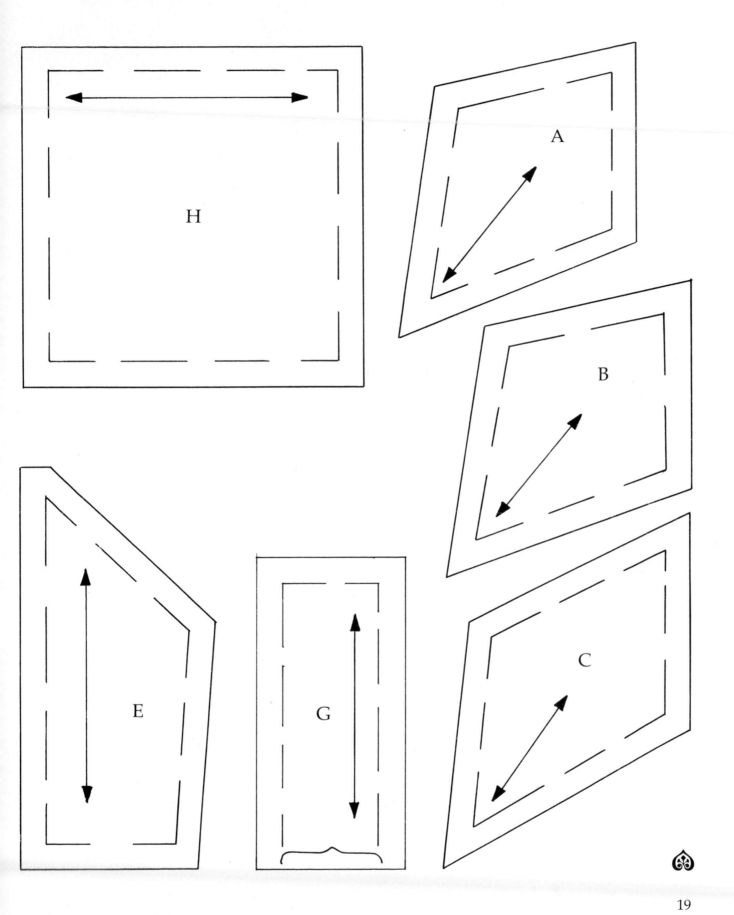

## BIRDS AND FLOWERS
Jamie McCauley Stephenson
LaFayette, Georgia

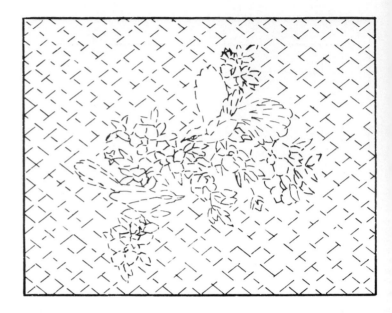

"Once upon a time a Cherokee Indian maiden fell in love with a Seminole brave from Florida. She married the brave and planned to return to Florida with him. She knew she would never see her father and the forests of Georgia again. Her father gave her a root from the rose that grew around the door of her home. She planted it in her new home to remind her of her home in Georgia.

"My husband and I moved to the country five years ago. As I wash dishes early in the morning, I have a view of the creek that runs parallel to our house. Quail browse up and down the creek bank, and a kingfisher stalks minnows from an old snag. Because of my love for quilts, birds, and the lovely Indian legend, it was only natural that I put them all together."

This spectacularly beautiful design is really more of a fabric painting than a regular quilt block. It makes a lovely banner when hung on the wall. It could, however, be used as the center design on a quilt top. The background quilting pattern of diagonal lines forming 1¼" (3.2cm) squares adds to the beauty of the design.

*Birds and Flowers* is difficult to make because each petal and each leaf, as well as each bird, is cut from a different pattern piece. For this reason, we have given you a drawing of the design to work from. Our suggestions for how to work are as follows:

1. Trace the drawing onto graph paper.
2. Enlarge the design to the desired size. Mrs. Stephenson's background rectangle measures 25½" x 21" (64.8cm x 53.3cm) without the border.

3. Trace the outline of each shape onto a separate sheet of paper.
4. Add seam allowances to each shape.
5. Cut each piece from fabric as it is needed, then stitch each in place.

Color key for drawing:
A—yellow
B—white
C—medium value green print
D—dark green
E—medium brown
F—brown with white print
G—white with brown print

Part of the effectiveness of this quilt block is the way it is bordered. The 2 brown and white prints from the central design are repeated, with the inside border slightly wider than the outer border. The inside strip is 1½" (3.8cm) wide, and the outer border is 1" (2.5cm) wide.

Details are embroidered as follows:
Birds' eyes—satin stitch and stem stitch in brown
Stems—chain stitch in green
Calyxes—satin stitch in green
Birds' legs—satin stitch and stem stitch in brown
Buds—satin stitch in white
Bud casings—lazy daisy or satin stitch in green

# CALICO BOUQUET

Mrs. Mamie Heasley
Little Rock, Arkansas

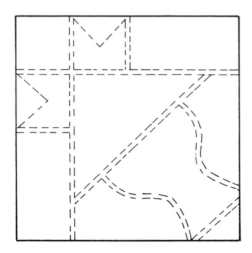

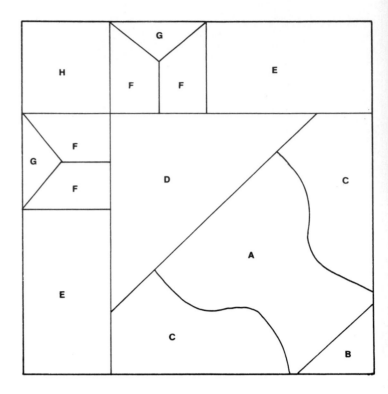

"Some of my earliest memories are of my mother making quilts. My first quilt, a *Nine Patch*, was made one cold winter when I was nine years old. After I married, it was used until it wore out.

"This quilt, *Calico Bouquet*, is adapted from one I remember my mother piecing in the early 1900s when I was very young. We have always grown flowers and had house plants, and this pattern reflects my liking for quilts and for flowers too.

"The 'calico' in the name refers not only to the fabric for the flowers in the quilt, but also to the small town in north Arkansas, Calico Rock, near where I was born, grew up, married, and lived until 1936.

"I have always drawn quilt patterns, and in the days when my children were young and commercial patterns were not easy to get, I made up and cut the patterns for their dresses, shirts, and overalls, and for my dresses, too."

Mrs. Heasley's charming patchwork design is one of our favorites. It repeats well, and because of its simplicity of line, the very gayest of colors and prints can be used.

Each finished block measures 9¼" (23.5cm) square.
One block takes the following:
A—1 vase
B—1 corner triangle for background
C—2 backgrounds for vase
D—1 large triangle for flower
E—2 background rectangles
F—4 trapezoids for flower
G—2 triangles for background
H—1 corner square for background

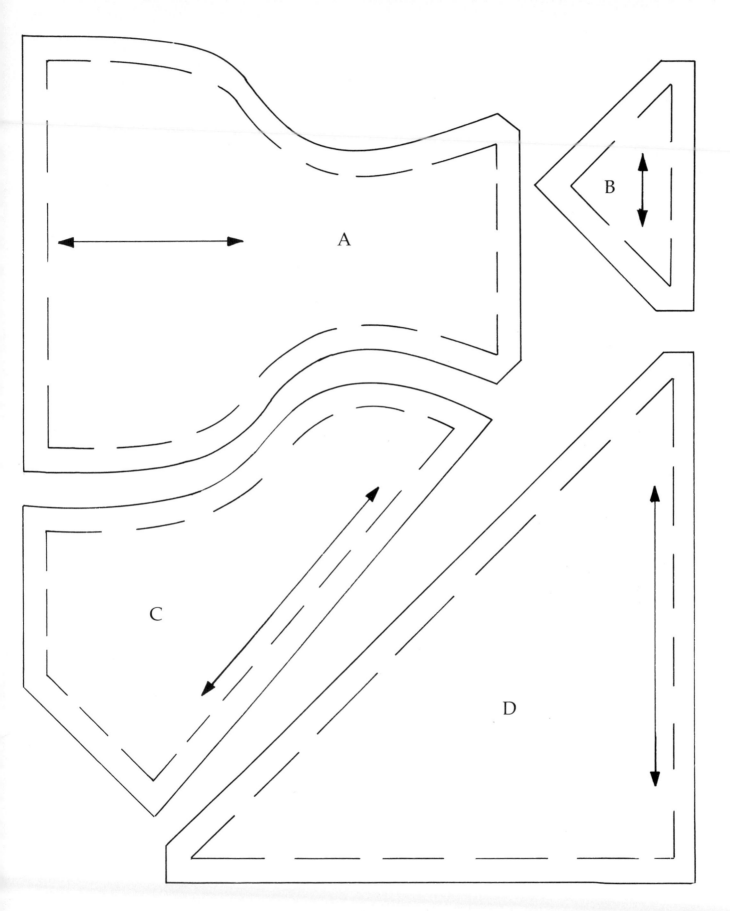

A

B

C

D

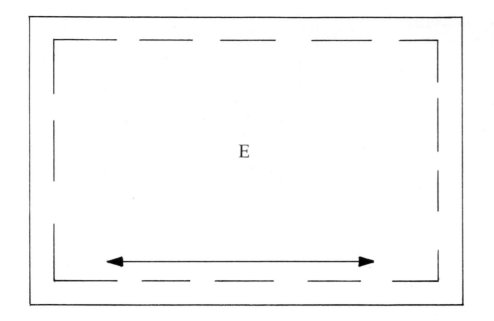

E

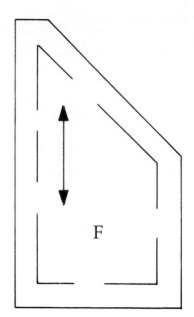

F

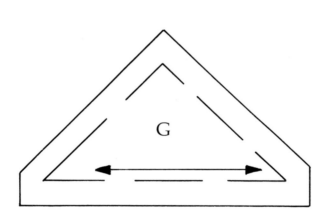

G

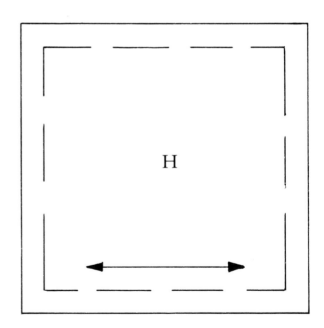

H

# CHEROKEE ROSE
Mrs. Clifford Westerfield
Athens, Georgia

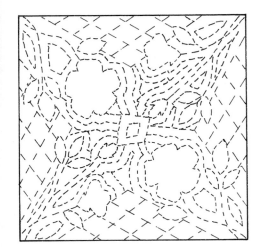

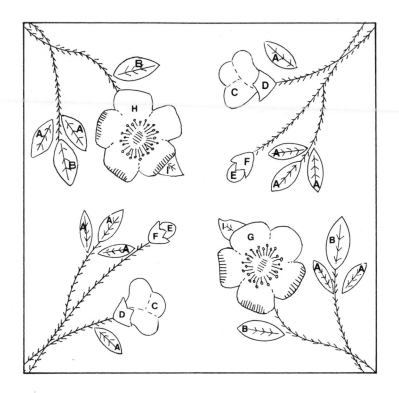

"I call this design *Cherokee Rose*. When the squares are placed together correctly, there will be a vining effect, similar to the way the Cherokee rose grows in its natural state. It also has a large number of briars, which I tried to imitate by combining the briar stitch with an outline stitch on the main stems.

"I think the Cherokee rose is a beautiful flower, and I am glad it was chosen for Georgia's state flower. That is why I picked it for my original quilt block design."

We, in turn, are glad that Mrs. Westerfield chose the Cherokee rose as the inspiration for her design, as it is one of the most beautiful and original we have seen. Although the appliqué and embroidery of each petal and flower require a certain amount of time and effort, it should be a pleasure to work up one block at a time.

Press light creases into the background block to divide it into even fourths, as an aid to positioning the leaves and flowers. Be careful that the vines are placed to match at the corners for the twining, rambling effect so necessary to the overall beauty of the quilt. See the photograph on page 3 for Mrs. Westerfield's idea of how the quilt should be bordered.

Each finished block measures 17" (43.2cm) square.

One block takes the following:
A—12 small leaves
B— 4 large leaves
C— 2 unopened blossoms
D— 2 calyxes for unopened blossoms
E— 2 buds
F— 2 calyxes for buds
G— 1 opened blossom
H— 1 opened blossom
I— 2 leaf tips
Background square—17½" x 17½" (44.5cm x 44.5cm)

*(Continued on following page)*

25

In addition to cutting each flower and leaf from the fabric you will use for appliqué, also cut each shape out of fiber fill or some other material to use for padding the design as you appliqué it in place.

Use an outline stitch to sew over all the edges, then highlight the edges of pieces G and H as indicated. Make the centers of G and H with a satin stitch, and surround the centers with the long and short stitch and French knots. Use a stem (outline) stitch to make veins on the leaves. The combination of stem and briar stitch is perfect for the vines.

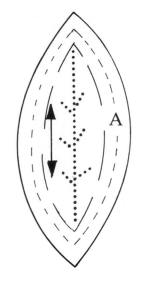

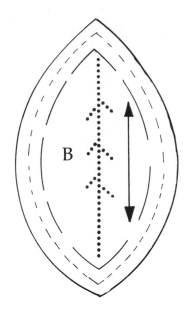

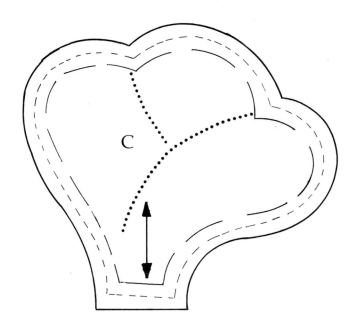

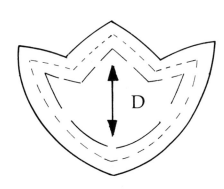

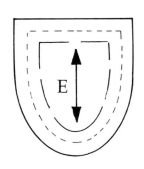

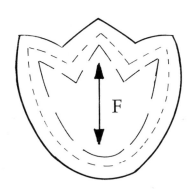

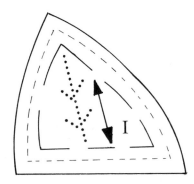

G

H

# DONKEY

Mrs. Jewel G. Jones
Bryan, Texas

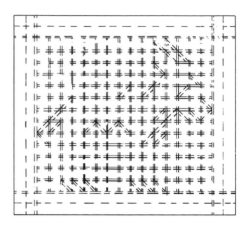

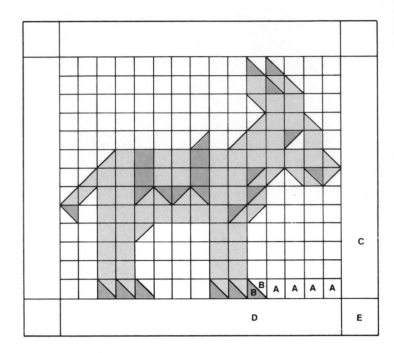

"The donkey, in addition to being man's beast of burden since Biblical times, has been perhaps one of the most important animals in the settlement and development of our country. In our area of central Texas, the donkey was used for everything from clearing and cultivating the rich Brazos bottom lands to the lowly chore of hauling the garbage at Texas A&M University. Donkeys were used by the Spanish in the early exploration and settlement of our southwest and were used in huge pack trains to move trade goods and riches across our country. The donkey was used by the prospector and the gold miner to exploit the riches of our nation. Donkeys were also used in the southwest in huge pack trains to move commodities and military supplies to many remote military outposts.

"Today, in an age when man has been on the moon, the donkey still serves us in time-honored ways. For example, in some of our national parks he is used both as a pack animal and as a sure-footed mount on steep narrow trails. The donkey may be one of the most stubborn creatures, but he is certainly one of the most sure-footed animals alive."

This variation on an old favorite design is based completely on a square and half-square, or triangle. The hardest part of this appealing patchwork design is counting the number of squares and triangles needed in each color. The central rectangle measures 28" (71.1cm) wide by 23½" (59.7cm) high. With the addition, as shown on page 7, of 3" (7.6cm) wide borders and corner squares, you have a quilted banner that is perfect for a child's room. A full-size quilt can be made by adding more solid-color squares to lengthen and widen the original block and also by making the borders wider.

One block takes the following:
A—110 white squares
      46 blue print squares
       4 red squares
B— 22 white triangles
      28 blue print triangles
      20 red triangles
The border takes the following:
C— 2 red side strips, $23\frac{1}{2}$" x $3\frac{1}{2}$"
     (59.7cm x 8.9cm)
D— 2 red top and bottom strips,
     $26\frac{3}{4}$" x $3\frac{1}{2}$" (67.9cm x 8.9cm)
E— 4 blue corner squares, $3\frac{1}{2}$" x
     $3\frac{1}{2}$" (8.9cm x 8.9cm)
Follow the piecing diagram care-
fully for correct placement of the
squares and triangles.

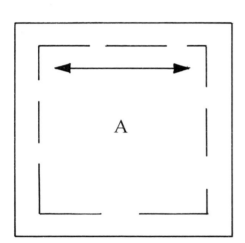

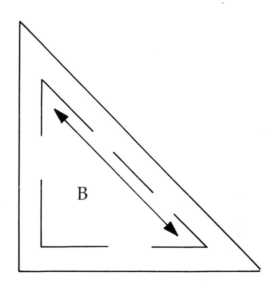

# EVERGREENS
Irene G. Harper
Evergreen, Alabama

"One of the benefits of living in Conecuh County near the county seat of Evergreen is that we have numerous different trees with beautiful leaves. Vines and shrubs also grow abundantly in the vicinity. Around 1895, there came to Evergreen a Canadian known as Caldwell the Woodsman, who saw the possibilities of a lucrative business in the shipping of smilax and other evergreens to northern markets. One of his first customers was the White House. When President Grover Cleveland married Frances Folsom, the White House was decorated with greenery shipped from Evergreen. This beginning—the idea of one man—later developed into one of the largest businesses of its kind in the South.

"This bit of history and the beauty and love of evergreens prompted me to design this square of leaves and vines."

Mrs. Harper has used several shades of green and many different leaf shapes to carry out the theme of her design. Her simplified, and to some extent abstract, leaf shapes are enhanced and repeated by the quilt-ing in the center of the large central circle. Of further interest are the smaller secondary circles that are formed at the corners when four squares join. Therefore, these squares should be set directly next to one another. Mrs. Harper suggests 20 squares, 4 across and 5 down, for a full-size quilt. Interesting possibilities for a beautiful border exist by adapting some of the curving vine and leaf shapes, very much as with *Cherokee Rose* on page 3.

Each finished block measures 20½" (52cm) square.

One block takes the following:
Leaf A— 4 light green
             4 dark green
Leaf B— 4 yellow print
Leaf C—24 dark green
Leaf D— 4 light green
             4 dark green
Dark green bias strips in a finished width of ¼" (6mm), cut to the following specifications:
4 pieces for corner stems, each 1¾" (4.4cm) long
4 pieces for corner circles, each 9½" (24.1cm) long

1 piece for center circle, 39½"
   (100.3cm) long
Background square—21" x 21"
   (53.3cm x 53.3cm)

To help in positioning pieces for appliqué, mark lightly the center circle, which has a diameter of 12" (30.5cm) on the right side of the fabric. Pin the tape for the center circle in place; then position the leaves. Mark 5" (12.7cm) in from each corner to determine where the bias tape for the corner circles should fall; then pin it in place. Position corner leaves according to the piecing diagram. Appliqué all pieces in place with a blind stitch. Embroider holly berries in center with a satin stitch.

*Special hint*: Bias strips may be shaped into circles and curves before placing on the background fabric by using a cardboard pattern of the desired diameter, lots of steam from a steam iron, and careful manipulation.

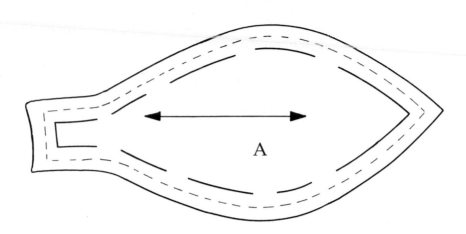

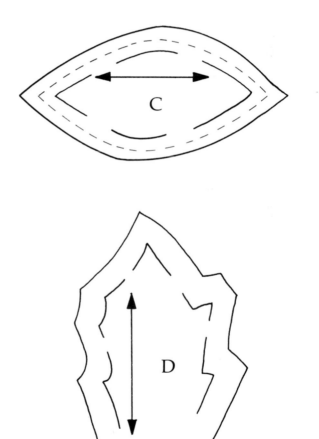

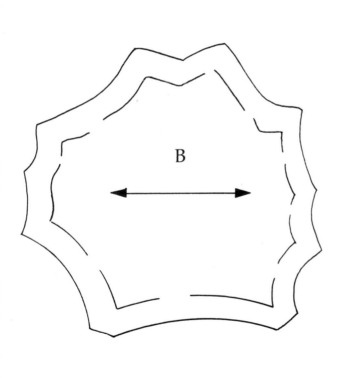

# FIELDS' LOST ACRE
Mrs. Clarice Fields
Bonnieville, Kentucky

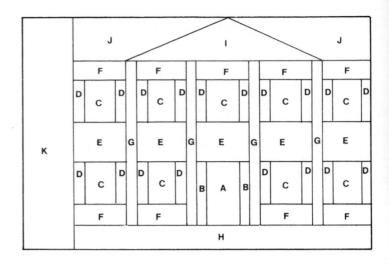

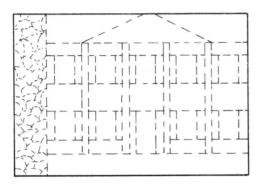

"In January, 1975, we bought a farm in Hart County. It had a house that was 100 years old. The back part that we tore down was even older than that. It had square nails in it. We kept the front part that had two rooms up and two rooms down. We dug a basement under where the old part was, finished it, and moved in. We will build a two story on top of the basement and attach it to the old part we kept. When we get through, we will have 10 rooms, 2½ baths, plus the finished basement and an attic room.

"The reason I call this pattern *Fields' Lost Acre* is that for several years no one has lived on the farm. It was so grown up with weeds and such that it looked lost and awful. Several people thought we were crazy to tackle anything this big, but we like to take nothing and make something out of it. We plan to do the reconstruction work ourselves. This quilt block is how our house will look when we are finished."

We wonder how Mrs. Fields has time to piece such an effective patchwork pattern when she's so busy fixing up the source of the design! A large quilt will benefit from sashing, and the detail drawing shows Mrs. Fields' suggestion for free-form quilted sashing. You can also see a section of sashing in the color photograph on page 7.

Each finished block measures 12" x 14" (30.5cm x 35.6cm).

One block takes the following:
A— 1 door
B— 2 door facings
C— 9 windows
D—18 window facings
E— 5 house fronts
F— 9 above and below window sections
G— 4 columns
H— 1 ground or porch
I— 1 gable
J— 2 backgrounds

The sashing strips (Piece K) Mrs. Fields used are 3½" (8.8cm) wide. Decide on the length needed for sashing across top and bottom of each row of blocks after you determine how wide the quilt will be.

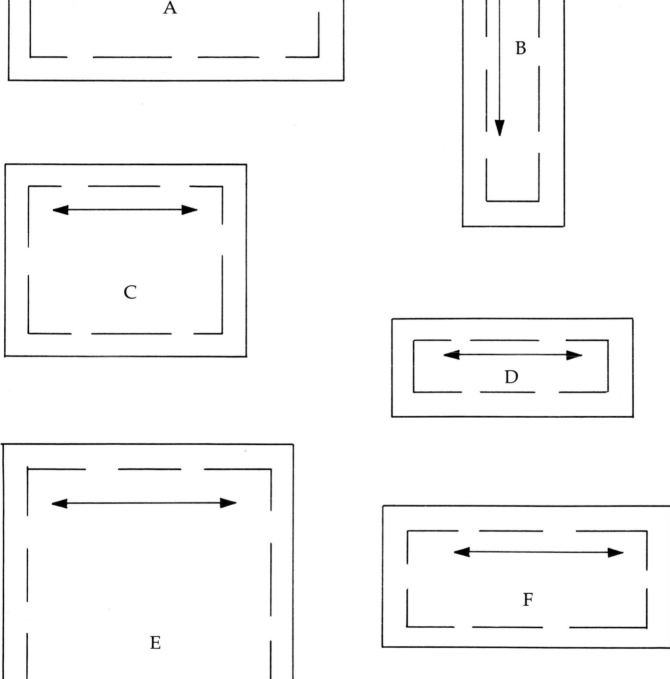

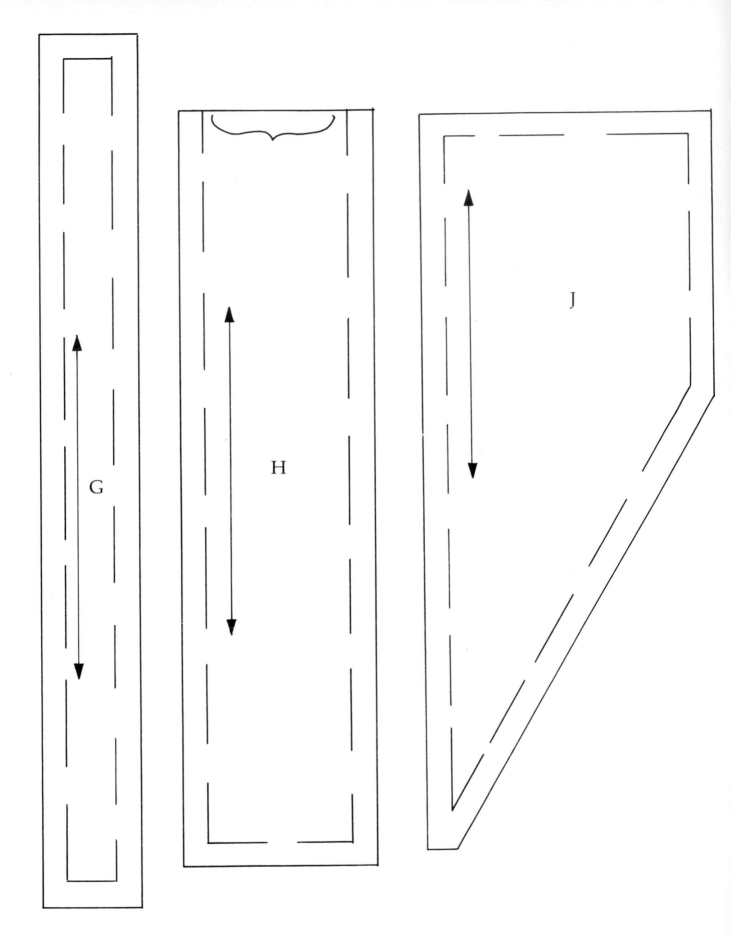

G

H

J

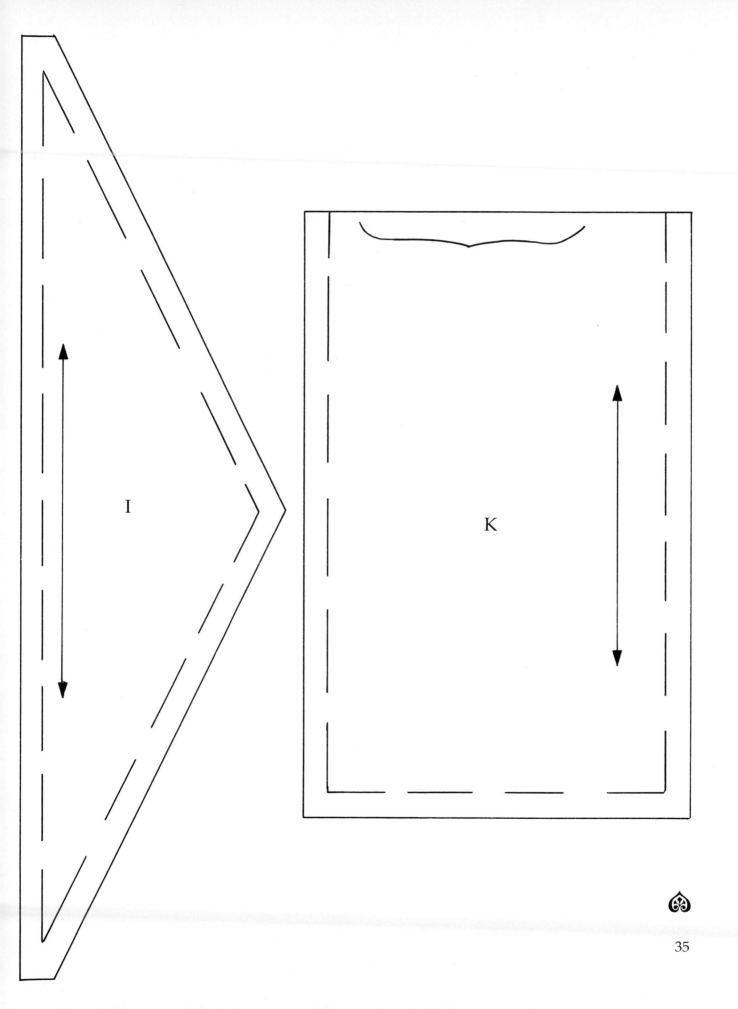

I

K

# GOD'S BOUNTY*

Sharon Shelley
East Ridge, Tennessee

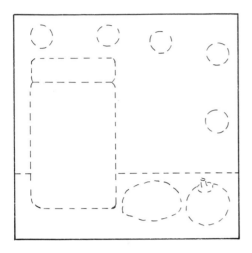

"I have tried to create with my design what a country kitchen table might look like during canning time. This design reminds me of my grandmother and the time she spent canning foods that would be used all year. A garden always seems, somehow, to provide for all the needs of a family, plus ample to share with others. Canned foods serve as a reminder all year long of God's goodness and the blessings He has bestowed."

This literal interpretation of familiar objects won the quilt contest judges' hearts, and they awarded it a special mention. It is a captivating design and would lend itself particularly well to small projects such as potholders, tea cozies, clothing, and the like. For a large quilt, this block should be used with other blocks portraying similar themes, each block set off with sashing to complement the overall design of the quilt.

Work on the block will go easily if the embroidery on the jar and the potato is stitched before each is

appliquéd in place. A combination of satin and stem (outline) stitches are used on the jar, and groups of straight stitches are used to make the eyes on the potato. (French knots would also work well on the potato.) The jar might be padded during appliqué. Notice that the portion of the tablecloth underneath the jar has been cut out to eliminate bulk.

Each finished block measures 10" (25.4cm) square.

One block takes the following:
A—1 tablecloth
B—1 jar
C—1 lid
D—1 potato
E—1 tomato
F—1 stem

---

*Judges' Choice

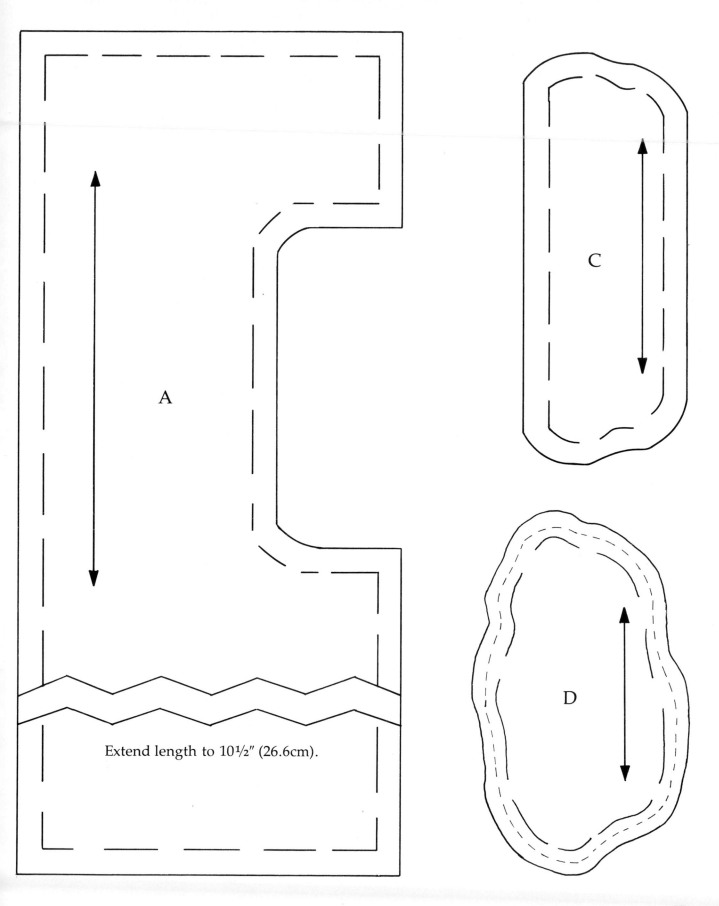

A

Extend length to 10½″ (26.6cm).

C

D

B

PERFECT MASON

F

E

38

# GREAT GRANDMA
Mrs. Velma H. Culbert
Beggs, Oklahoma

"This design truly depicts our Southern rural heritage. It was designed for that very purpose, to portray some of the most blessed experiences of country living. I have made twelve or more designs for this *Great Grandma* quilt, and it wasn't easy to select the right one for the contest. The designs depict activities of a farm; they show great grandma at work in the garden, plowing with a push plow, hoeing vegetables, pulling a little red wagon, carrying a great big pumpkin, building a rock garden, picking flowers, and feeding the chickens. What else better captures the essence of our Southern rural heritage than the everyday activities down on the farm?"

We don't know of anything more typical of Southern rural heritage than some of the scenes Mrs. Culbert so skillfully illustrates in her quilt. Be sure to refer to page 12 to see other of the quilt blocks she describes set into a quilt. Mrs. Culbert chose the design of the great grandma feeding the chickens to share with us, and it displays a lively folk-art quality. The fabric pieces are appliquéd in place,

then highlighted with embroidery stitches. This one square, used alone, makes a delightful fabric painting.

One block takes the following:

One of each pattern piece, with the following exceptions:

  A—2 hands

  B—3 leaves

Background square—18" x 18"
  (45.7cm x 45.7cm)

Embroidery stitches are as follows:

Bonnet—outline (stem) and
  straight stitch

Birds—satin and outline stitch

Chickens—satin and outline stitch

Apron—tied cross stitch

Chicken feed—French knots

Basket handle—outline stitch

Detail of arms and feet—outline
  stitch

Grass—outline stitch

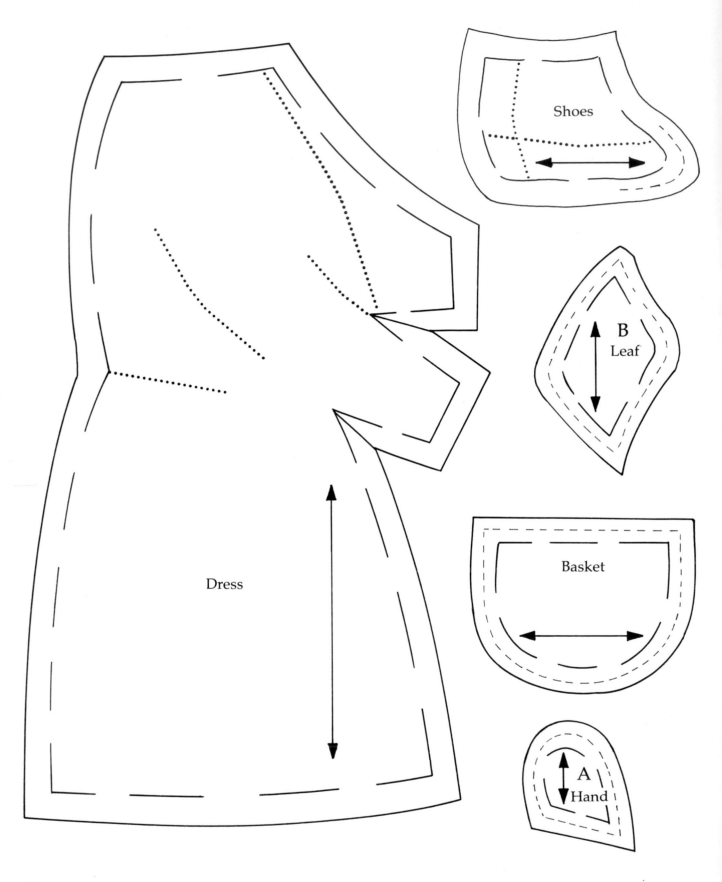

Shoes

B
Leaf

Dress

Basket

A
Hand

40

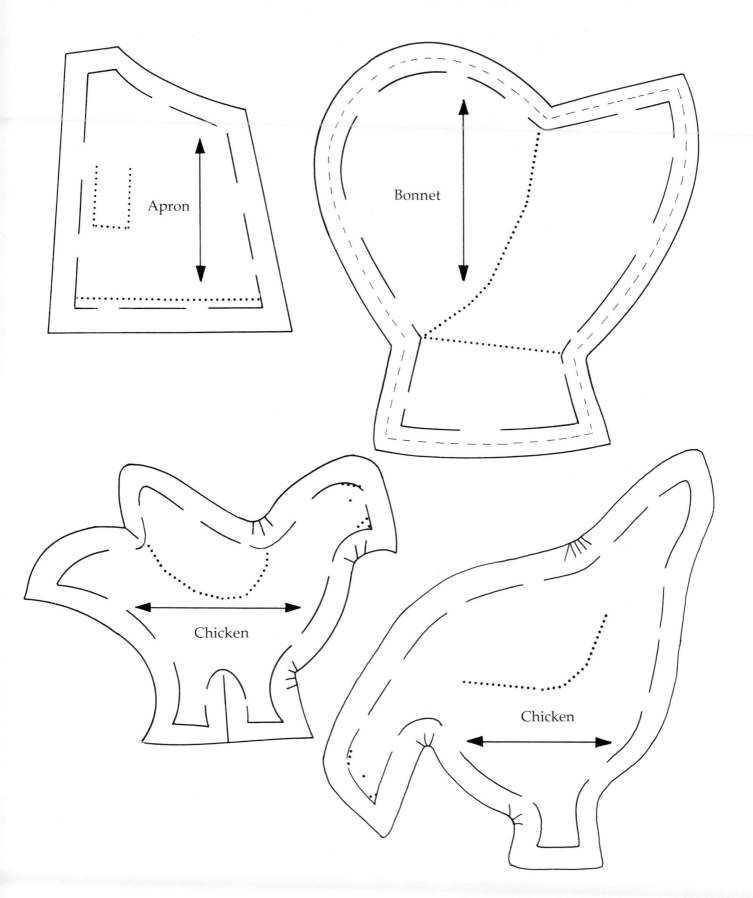

Apron

Bonnet

Chicken

Chicken

41

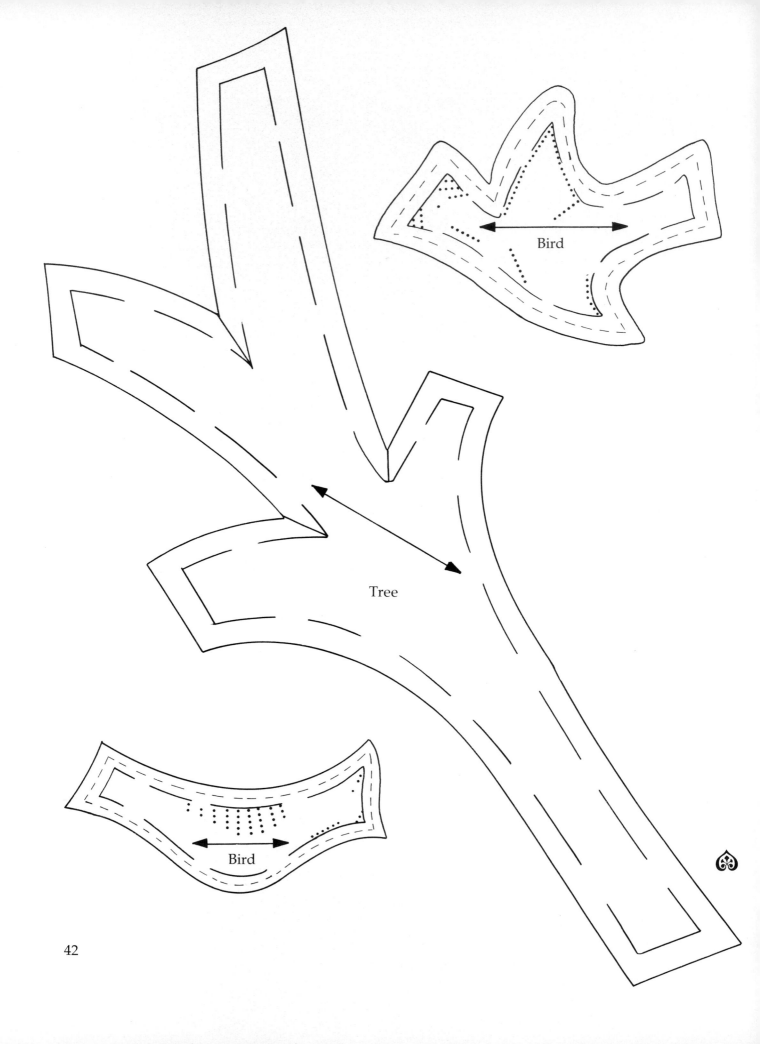

Bird

Tree

Bird

42

# GREEN IT UP AGAIN

Mrs. Margaret L. Beckman
Swanton, Maryland

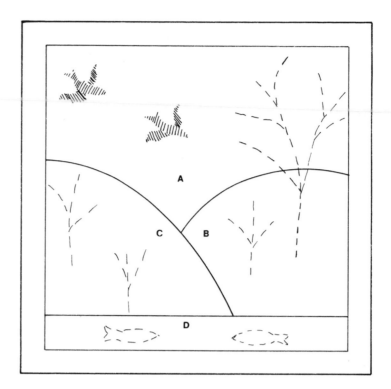

"Strip mining for coal in Garrett County inspired me to put this design in fabric. Nothing is more upsetting to our mountain heritage than to see so much brown earth over the countryside."

This touching plea to allow a return of beauty to a well-loved vista is a reminder that many emotions were recorded by our foremothers as they, too, saw changes in their environment and social conditions. The most natural form of expression for them was their quilting, and some of the most interesting historical recording was done with a needle and thread. Mrs. Beckman continues that tradition with her quilt block. We would suggest that you consider adapting her idea if you have a special project of your own that needs promoting—a humane society, or your local zoo, for example. The technique, because it is quilting, will attract attention to your message.

Each finished block measures 11½" (28.2cm) square. It is appliquéd and embroidered.

One block takes the following:
One of each pattern piece
Background square—12" x 12"
 (30.5cm x 30.5cm)

Appliqué each piece in place; then embroider the birds with a satin stitch and the trees with an outline (stem) stitch. Notice that some of the trees and the fish are formed by quilting stitches.

43

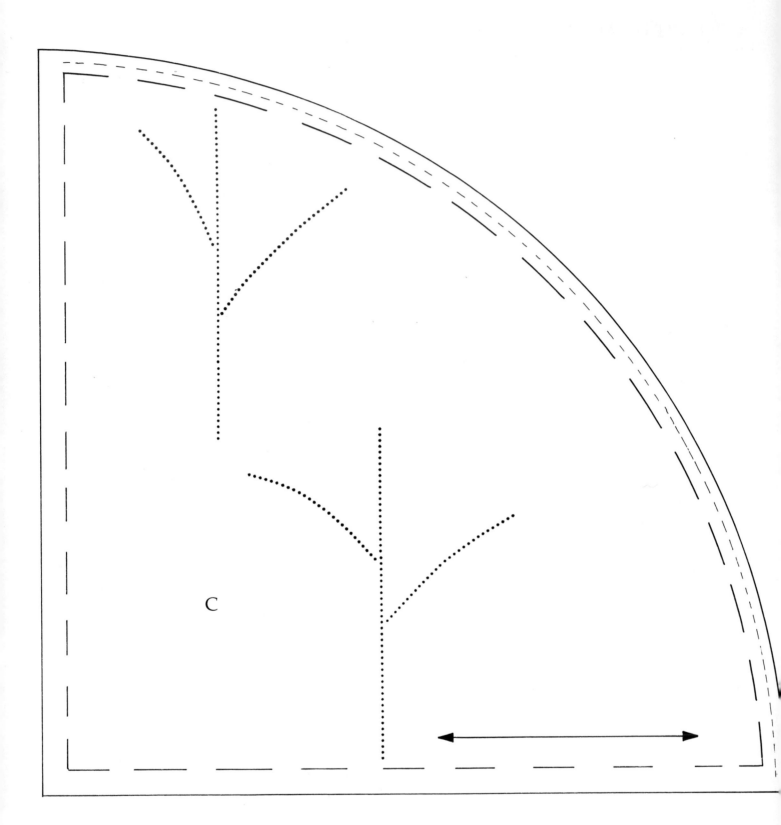

C

44

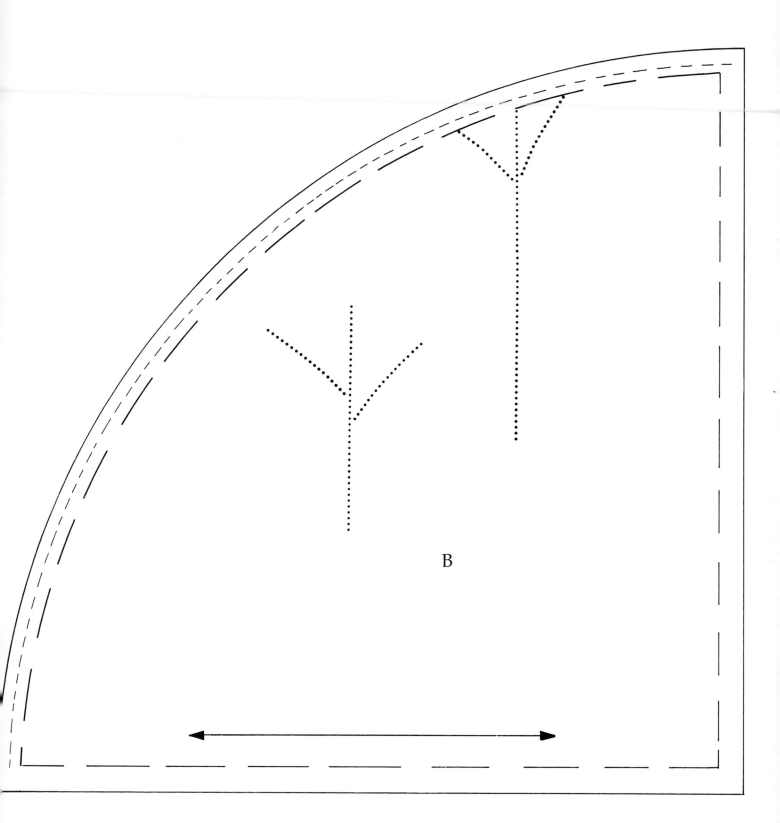

B

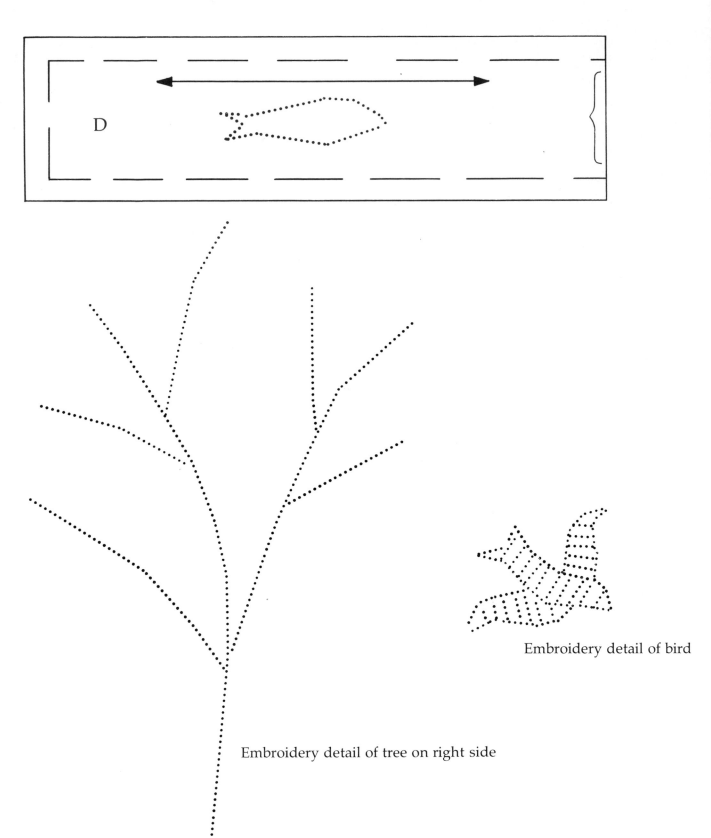

D

Embroidery detail of bird

Embroidery detail of tree on right side

46

# LOG SCHOOLHOUSE
Mrs. Fred O'Neal
Mt. Airy, North Carolina

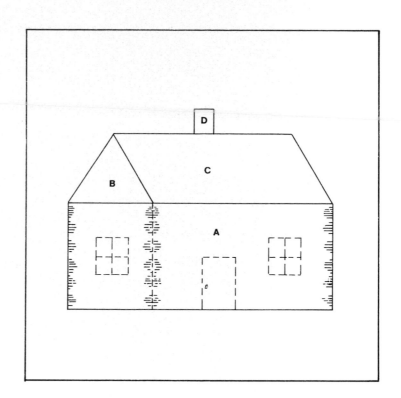

"As I designed this pattern, my mind wandered back to the days of long ago when I went to a school that was only one room. Built of logs from the nearby mountainsides, it was heated by a wood stove with logs gathered by the students. It seems almost like a dream to me now. So, I have drawn and quilted this pattern as I see it now in my dreams. I am 66 years old and love pretty things."

There are many schoolhouse quilt patterns in existence, but this one is unusual in that it is appliquéd, easy to do, and the "logs" are defined by quilting stitches and satin-stitched ends. The diagonal quilting of the roof adds to the strength of the design. Mrs. O'Neal's color scheme is also unique and quite effective (see page 8).

One block takes the following:
One of each pattern piece
Background square—13" x 13" (33cm x 33cm)
The doors and windows are defined with a twisted outline (stem) stitch. The ends of the logs and the doorknob are satin stitch.

This quilt pattern benefits from well-designed sashing and borders and would also be a nice contrast to solid squares displaying skilled geometric quilting.

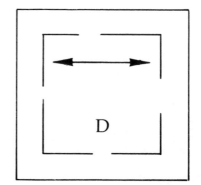

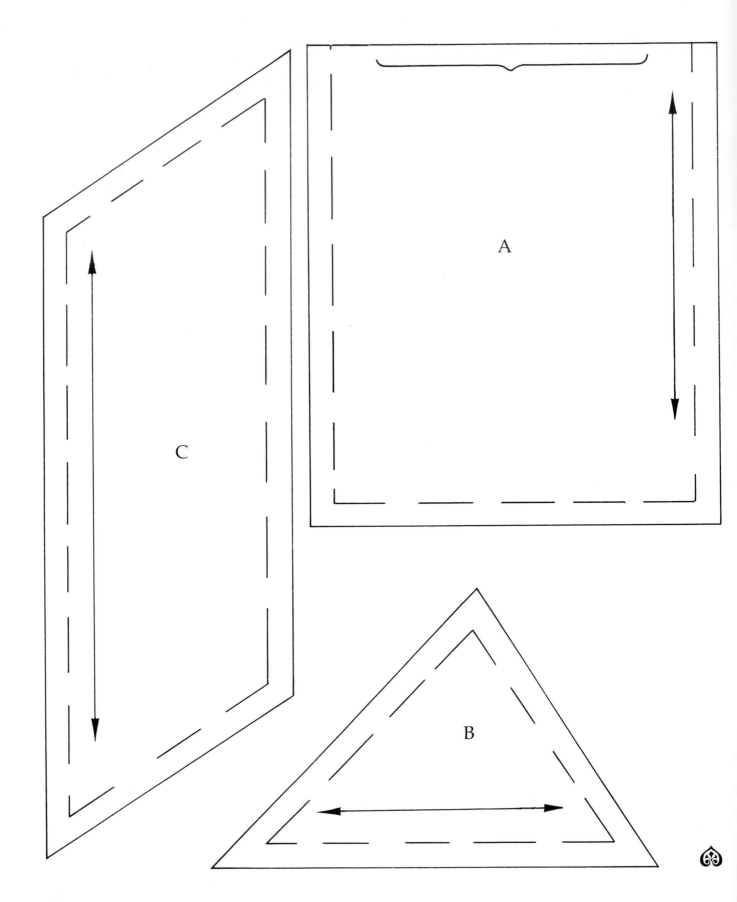

A

C

B

# MAGNOLIA BLOSSOM
Marceil Jones
Quitman, Arkansas

"America's South can boast of many beautiful things, but nothing can compare with the beauty of the magnificent magnolia tree. Its year-round beauty puts it in a class all its own. In the spring, the large, white, waxy blossoms with a yellow, conelike center appear at the ends of branches and last on into early summer. With the arrival of fall, the magnolia displays a beautiful red, seed-studded cone that is also attractive to many birds. In winter, its large, glossy, dark green, oval-shaped leaves growing in clusters are a welcome sight. The branches are used extensively in Christmas decorations.

"I've searched through many quilt pattern books to try to find an appliqué pattern for the magnolia blossom, but to no avail. So I've tried myself to capture some of the beauty of the glorious magnolia blossom."

This beautiful design is a bit difficult to construct, as each petal and leaf is cut from a different pattern piece. The diagonal quilting that forms ¾" (1.9cm) squares is a nice contrast to the gracefulness of the flower. A stem (outline) stitch in embroidery floss is used for detailing down the center of the leaves.

For one block you will need one of each of the pieces A through Q and a 14½" (36.8cm) background square. (This will give you a finished size of 14" [35.6cm]).

This block will repeat well for a full quilt, or it will combine beautifully with other flower designs. Sashing, perhaps in a leaf design, would accentuate the blocks.

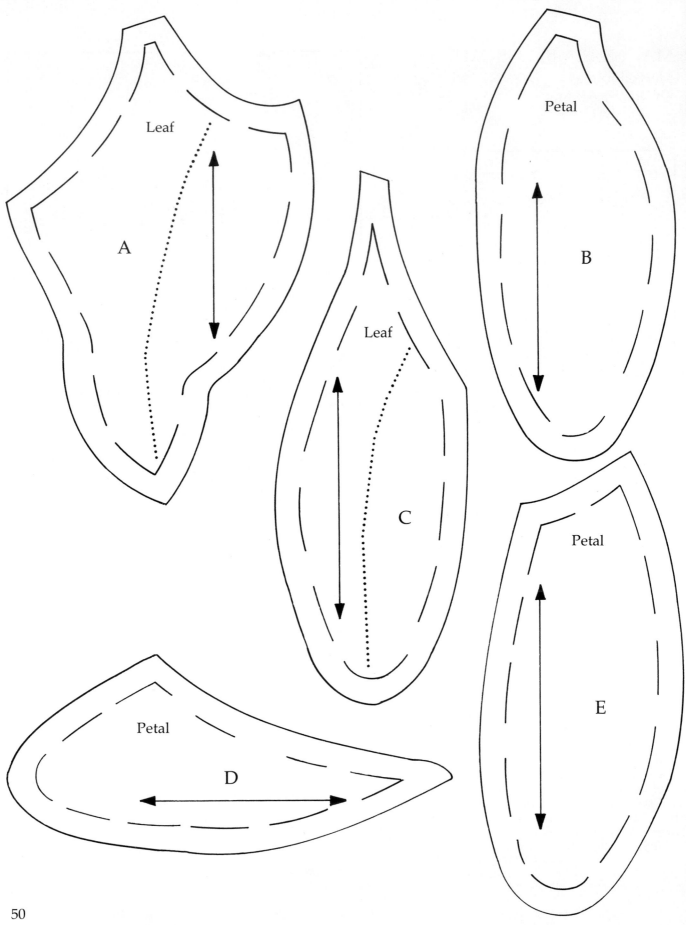

Leaf

A

Petal

B

Leaf

C

Petal

D

Petal

E

50

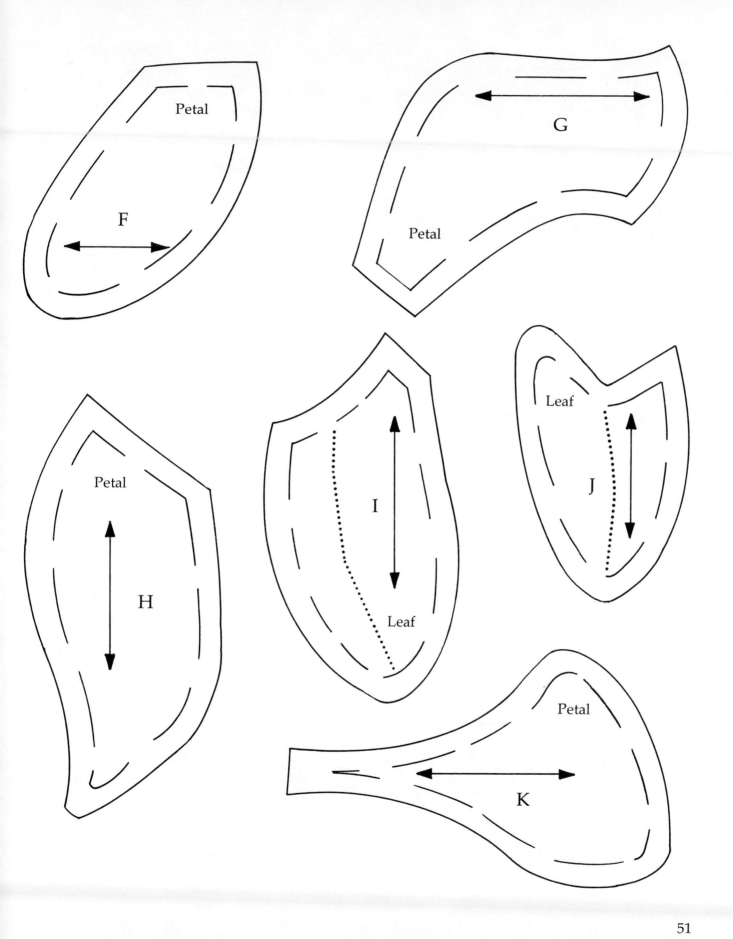

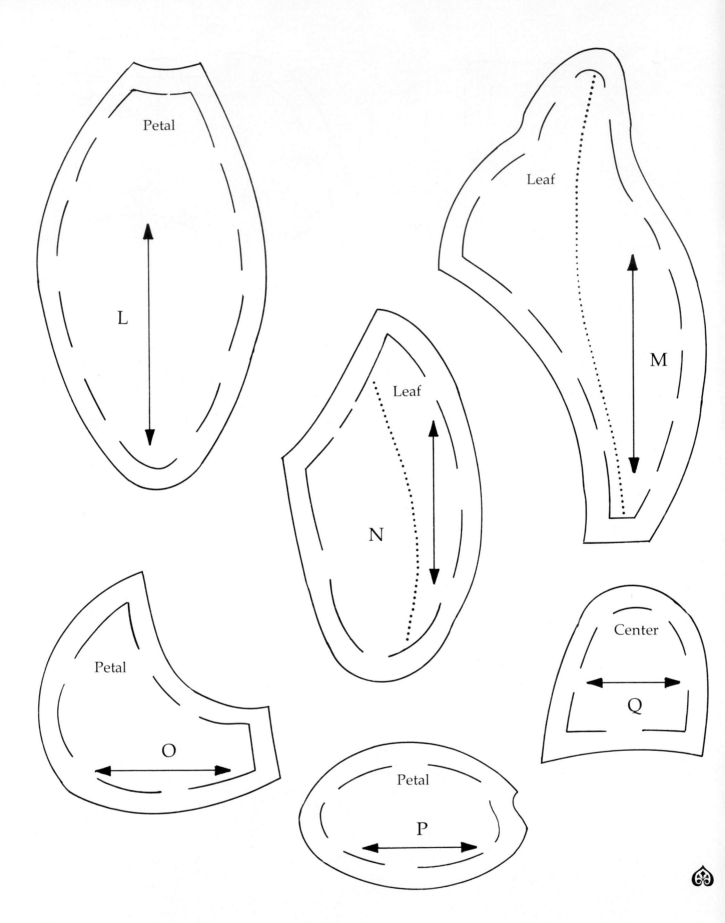

# MY GRANDMOTHER'S ROSE
Reta Ward
McDade, Texas

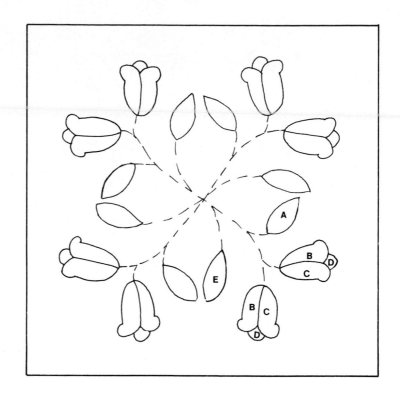

"Over 100 years ago, a young bride planted a rose bush in front of her log cabin in Texas and six children grew up loving the little rose. In the early 1900s the youngest son took over the farm. The log cabin was turned into a hay barn, and the little rose was trampled by the cattle and choked by weeds and grass. Several years later, the son was working around the old cabin when he spotted the little rose trying to bloom. Remembering all the joy the little rose had given the family, he dug it up and planted it in the yard of his new farm. When he got old and had to sell the farm, one of the things he moved to his new home was the little rose.

"The son was my grandfather; he is gone now, and I am a grandmother and the keeper of my great-grandmother's little pink rose.

"I feel Americans are like this rose. We may be uprooted, moved about, and choked by the weeds of life, but we have a good root system based on God, and we will survive and bloom in season."

The appliquéd pattern is lovely in its simplicity and is relatively easy to sew. The stems of the roses are made with a chain stitch, and the center of the leaves are defined with a quilting stitch. Sashing and a border of perhaps two fabrics in a 3" (7.6cm) width would be a nice complement to this design.

Each finished block measures 15½" (39.4cm) square.

One block takes the following:
A—4 leaves
B—8 outer petals
C—8 inner petals
D—8 buds
E—4 leaves
Background square—16" x 16" (40.6cm x 40.6cm)

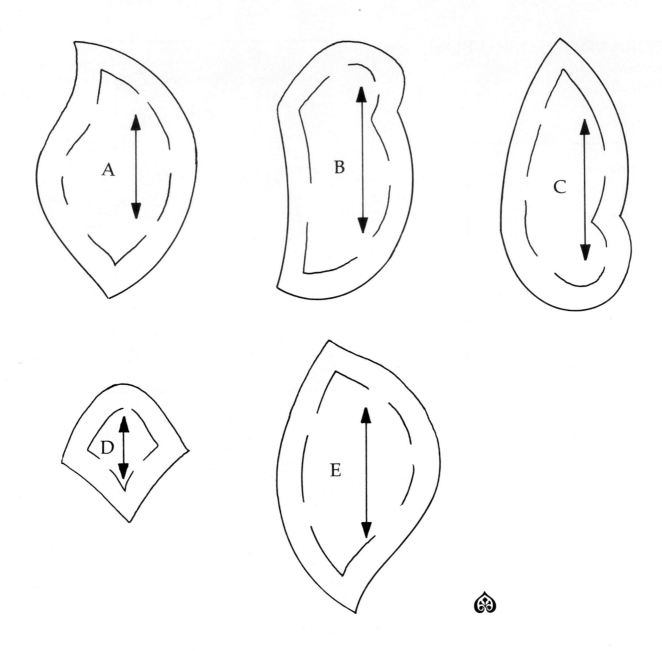

# NO NAME
Jane P. Howard
Pineville, Kentucky

Because of the age of this pattern, Mrs. Howard does not have much information about it. She adapted the design from a quilt believed to be 150 years old. The old, original quilt was shown to Mrs. Howard by a lady who lived to be 104. Mrs. Howard made her first quilt by this pattern 50 years ago and says the quilt is now worn out from use.

This extremely attractive appliqué flower pattern abounds with interesting details. The shaping of the petals is unusual, and the leaf quilting in the open areas enhances the design. The saw-tooth patchwork border provides an interesting geometric counterpoint. This border will become the sashing for the quilt.

*Special hint:* Remember that when the quilt blocks are set together, they share sashing with the adjoining blocks; therefore, sashing is required on only two adjoining sides of each block except the ones used in the last row of the quilt. The blocks in the last row require sashing on all four sides.

The flower is appliquéd onto a background square of 14" (35.6cm). The border measures 1½" (3.8cm) finished.

Each finished block measures 17" (43.2cm) square.
One block, bordered on all four sides, takes the following:
A— 1 flower center
B— 6 inner petals
C— 6 outer petals
D— 1 stem
E— 7 leaves
F—72 triangles total:
    36 print
    36 solid
Background square—14½" x 14½"
    (36.8cm x 36.8cm)

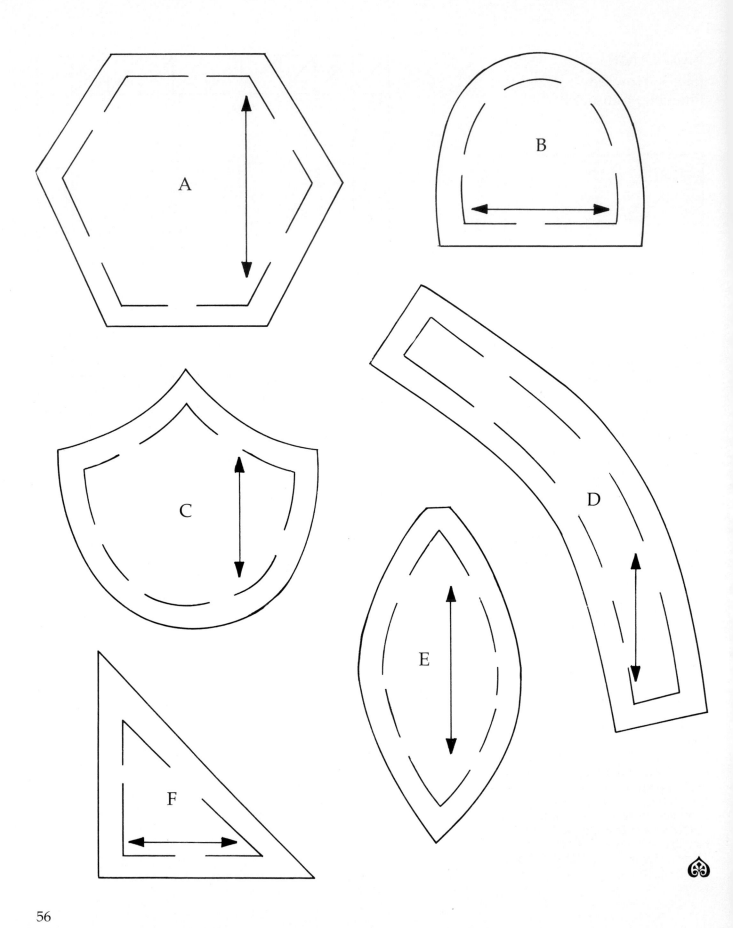

A

B

C

D

E

F

56

# PIONEER APPLE

Bessie T. Bagwell
Bankston, Alabama

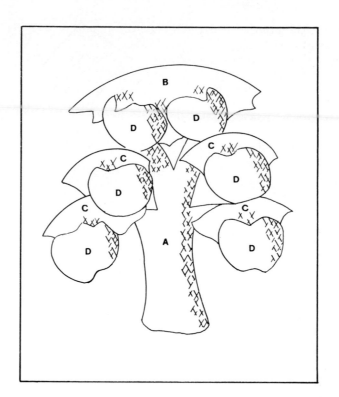

"In the early 1800s my maternal great-great-grandfather came to Alabama from North Carolina bringing his family and possessions. He brought with him apple sprouts, which he planted, and they thrived.

"Those apples inspired my quilt design. It is a special variety of apple that ripens in July. It is light yellow in color and has a very thin peel. It is unique in that although it gets very mellow, it still retains a very tart flavor.

"Great-Great-Grandfather passed on sprouts of this apple to each of his children when they married, so from his generation until now this apple has always been a part of my heritage. As a child I climbed the tree's branches, and I remember Grandma's back porch being filled with the fragrance of these apples in the summer.

"I can't speak for former generations, but on occasion my mother used a switch from this apple tree to put a wayward child back on the 'straight and narrow' path.

"Like Great-Great-Grandpa's posterity, his apple tree has lived and thrived in Alabama soil to this day. The six apples on my quilt block are for the six generations from Great-Great-Grandpa through my child. I used the gingham checks because I remember my own grandma always wearing neat little dresses made of gingham."

A variety of techniques combine to make this little apple tree a very interesting pattern to sew. Each apple is stuffed, or raised, with quilt batting before being appliquéd in place. The leafy boughs are slit so that the apples can be placed naturally in the green leaves; the slits are then stitched down with a buttonhole stitch. All the outer edges of each piece are finished with the buttonhole stitch. Highlighting and shadowing are provided by cross stitching. Grass is indicated by quilting stitches. Nothing is difficult, and it's lots of fun!

*(Continued on following page)*

Each finished block measures 13" x 15½" (33cm x 39.4cm).
   One block takes the following:
   A—1 tree trunk
   B—1 upper leaf section
   C—4 lower leaf sections
   D—6 apples
   Background rectangle—13½" x 16"
       (34.3cm x 40.6cm)

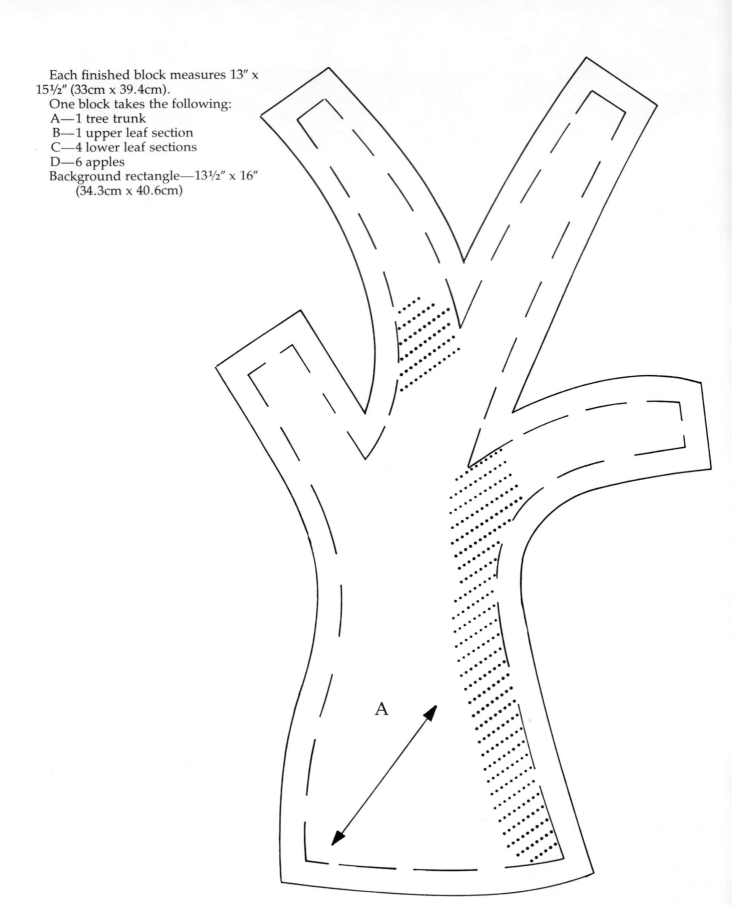

A

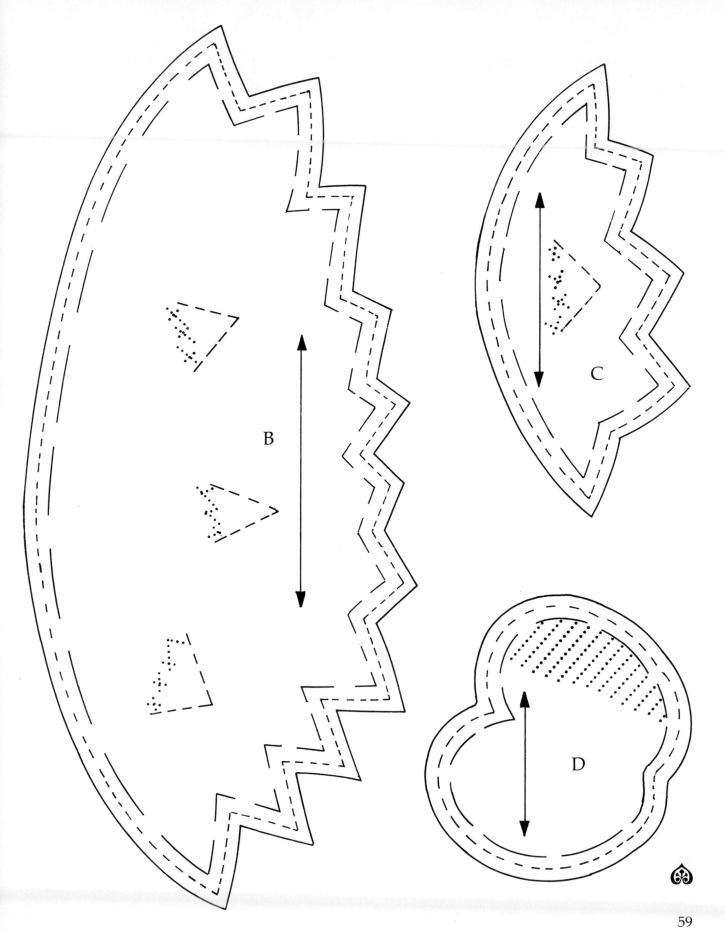

B

C

D

59

# SOUTH'S PRIDE DAISY
Mata J. G. Banks
New Tazewell, Tennessee

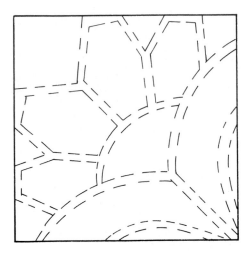

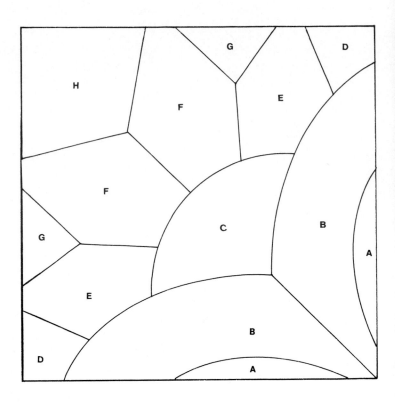

"Choosing a design motif which exemplified my rural heritage seemed like a large task. I chose something which is quite small but very abundant in the South: the field daisy, commonly called black-eyed Susan. Because I live just ten miles from Cumberland Gap and less than a day's ride from the Smokey Mountains, I considered using one of these as a theme; I felt, though, that they had already and often been praised. I turned slowly to the smaller and more unrealized beauty of the black-eyed Susan. I could see in it a symbol of the true South: simple but beautiful, standing tall into the sun and free to be enjoyed. Because it grows wild in most of the South, most people pass it by as though it were a mere weed. I feel that we should realize the flower is not just a weed, but a special flower picked by God to show the 'South's Pride.' "

Everything about this patchwork design contributes to its overall charm and spirit. There is a wonderful balance of straight and curved lines, a nice interplay of print and solid fabrics, and the colors Mrs. Banks used for her original block (see page 10) are the brightest and cheeriest available. This is surely one of the best abstract geometric flower designs there is. The daisy blocks would look best set on the diagonal and alternated with solid calico squares to match the background of this block.

Each finished block measures 11" (27.9cm) square.

One block takes the following:
A—2 backgrounds
B—2 leaves
C—1 center
D—2 backgrounds
E—2 petals
F—2 petals
G—2 backgrounds
H—1 background

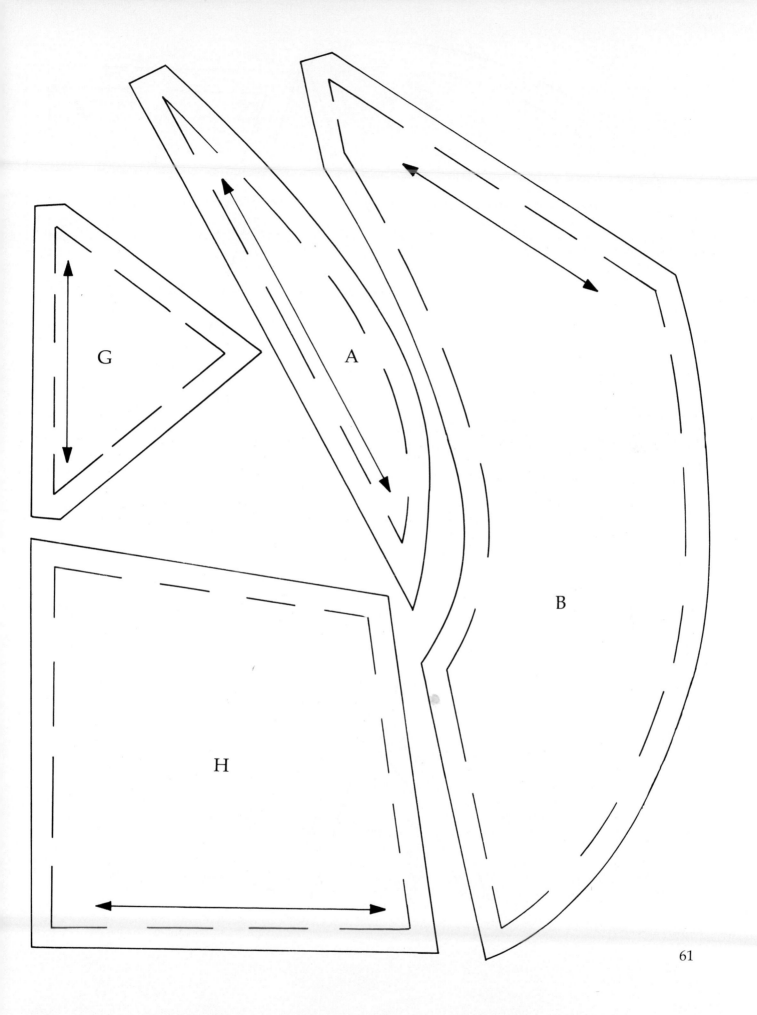

G

A

B

H

61

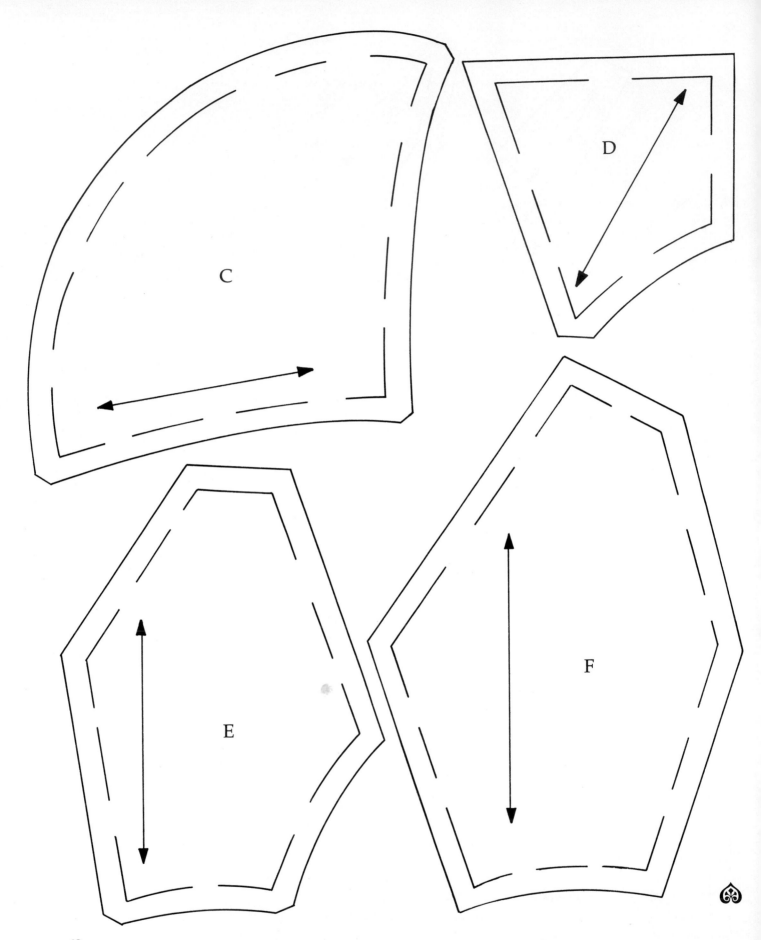

62

# SWEETHEART
Nancy J. Richardson
Zephyrhills, Florida

"I made the design and cut the pattern for this quilt in 1935. We had a community organization called the Stitch & Chatter Club. We met each month in our homes. The husbands were invited to eat with us, and they chatted while we stitched. Years later I heard of a *Sweetheart* quilt similar to the one I had designed but the hearts were broader, the background squares larger, and it had no sashing. It made a pretty quilt, but I have stuck to my own design.

"When I see my *Sweetheart* quilt I think of my friends of the Stitch & Chatter Club. Some people when they see my quilt tops say, 'Oh, a Valentine quilt.' It could be called that, but my first thought was *Sweetheart*. In my old age I am making quilts again as a hobby. I have five tops made and blocks for three more. Lots more quilting to do yet."

This utterly charming design can be made in endless combinations of fabrics. It is all appliqué and is easily sewed up. The outer edges of all the shapes are outlined with a running stitch. This quilt is particularly suited to the apartment quilting technique.

Each finished block measures 13" (33cm) square.
One block takes the following:
A—1 center (in same fabric as corners)
B—4 corner sections
C—4 hearts
Background square—13½" x 13½" (34.3cm x 34.3cm)
Quilt may be sashed with 2" (5cm) wide sashing.

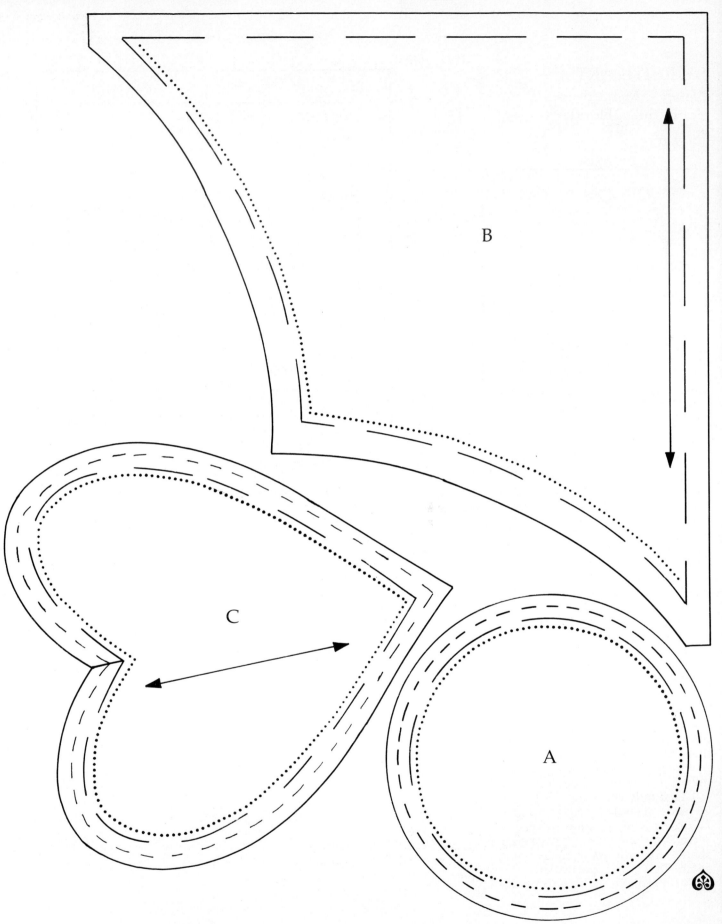

A

B

C

# TINY STARS AND SQUARES

Mrs. Laura S. Harris
Grantsboro, North Carolina

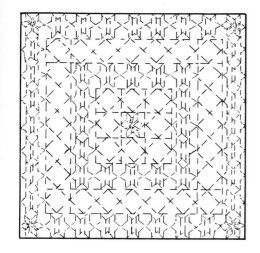

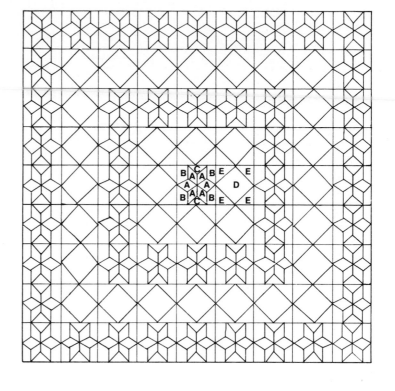

"I could think of nothing any prettier than the bright and shining stars at night. I have been a star watcher all my life. When I was a little girl, I almost wore out the song called 'Twinkle, Twinkle, Little Star.'

"So here is what I have come up with. It takes a little time and patience to piece this quilt, but it is worth it."

Mrs. Harris is right when she says it takes a little time and patience to piece this quilt. Each of the star blocks is made of 6 precisely fitted diamonds, with 6 surrounding pieces. Even the squares are set on the diagonal, requiring that the corners be pieced. She is also right, however, when she says that the work is worth it. This quilt design is illustrative of two of the most basic of patchwork traditions: it utilizes the tiniest of fabric scraps; and, because it is practically self-repeating, it can be made to exactly the required size without compromising the design. The regularity of the design serves to unify even the widest variety of printed fabrics. However, you should follow Mrs. Harris' idea and put dark backgrounds on all the stars and light backgrounds on all the squares.

Each finished star block measures 2½" (6.4cm) square.

One star block takes the following:

A—6 diamonds
B—4 trapezoids
C—2 triangles

Each finished square block measures 2¼" (5.7cm) square.

One square block takes the following:

D—1 square
E—4 triangles

You must figure how many of each block you will need for your project. The large square illustrated on page 10 took 49 star blocks and 32 square blocks.

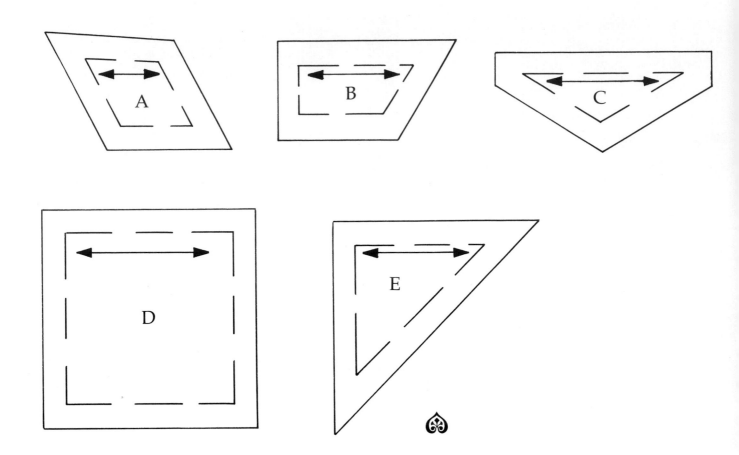

# TRACTOR PULL
Mrs. Douglas Dorhauer
Denham Springs, Louisiana

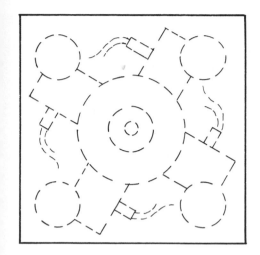

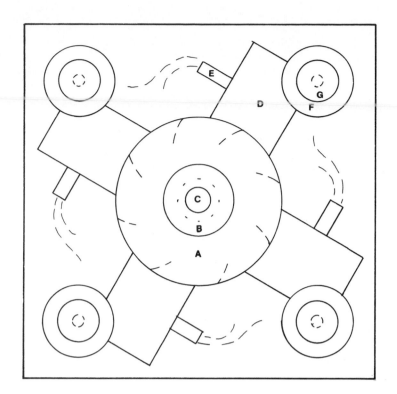

"We have a small farm and my husband uses the tractor for all kinds of farm work. Our little boy has his own toy riding tractor. Even I get on the tractor once or twice a year to break up ground for my spring and fall garden.

"But that fun-loving, competitive spirit in most Americans couldn't let the tractor be just a workhorse. Therefore, the tractor pull came into existence. Although we have never attended one, our neighbor, a dairyman with a big tractor of his own, tells us about the excitement that goes on there. In my mind I can see those big machines tugging weights in contest against one another. From this I drew my idea for my appliquéd quilt pattern. I suggest using a different color for each tractor. This would be a fine quilt for a little boy's room."

This design is one of the most unique in appearance and interesting in execution that we have seen. Mrs. Dorhauer padded and tucked the wheel to make it very realistic in appearance. A sashing in a print fabric would be a nice contrast to the solid fabrics of the quilt block.

Each finished block measures 14" (35.6cm) square.
One block takes the following:
A—1 large wheel (mark placement of tucks on right side of fabric)
B—1 hub
C—1 axle
D—4 tractor bodies
E—4 smoke stacks
F—4 front wheels
G—4 front hubs
Background square—14½" x 14½" (36.8cm x 36.8cm)

To make the center wheel, appliqué C to B, then B to A. Stitch the tucks on the right side of the wheel. Mrs. Dorhauer used contrasting thread for the tucks. Gather outer edge of A slightly and turn under seam allowance. Pin A to center of background square. Stuff the wheel, but do not stitch around outer edge until tractor bodies have been sewed in place.

French knots are used to make the big nuts in the center wheel. A satin stitch is used for the axle of the front wheel, and the stem (outline) stitch makes the trails of smoke.

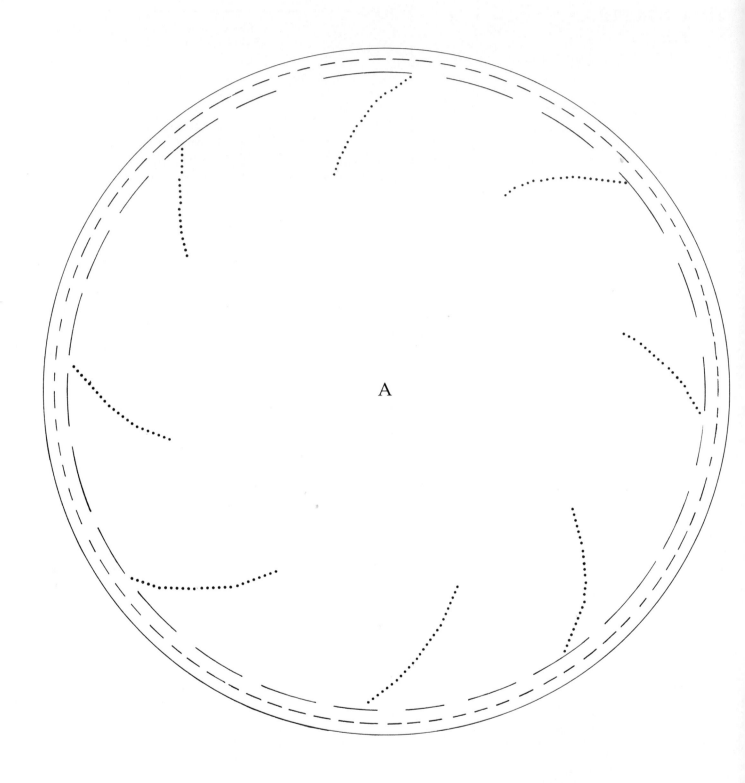

A

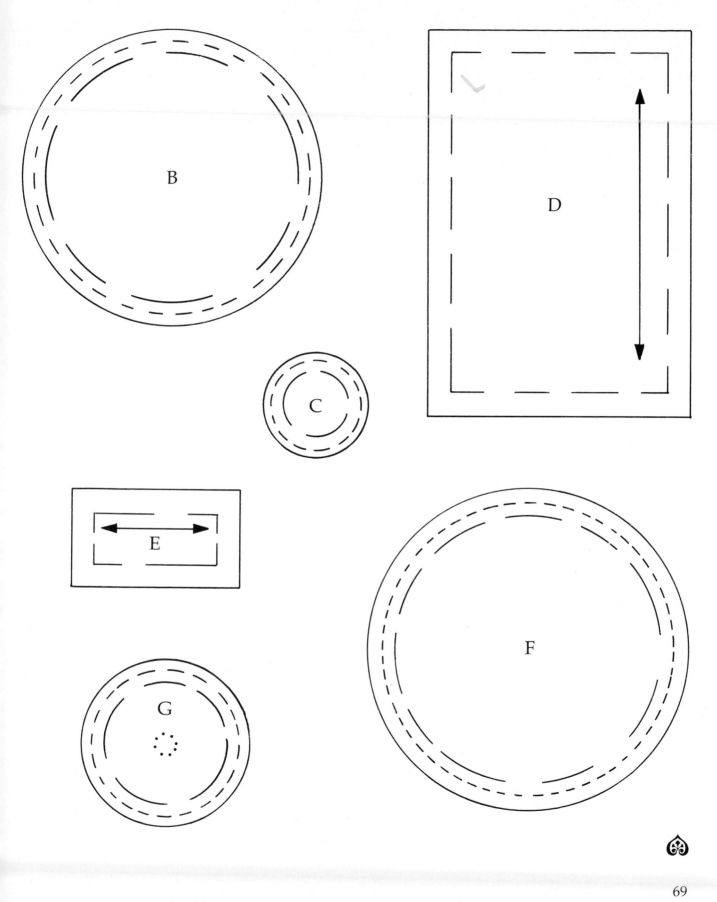

B

D

C

E

F

G

# TRANQUILITY
Clio D. Niebauer
Pittsburgh, Pennsylvania

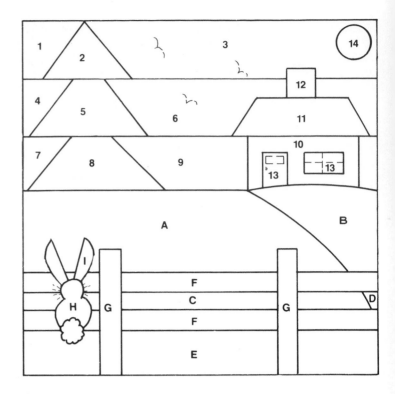

"The word 'tranquility' means peaceful, quiet and serene. These words describe our family farm in Tennessee where I spent the first 20 years of my life. The farm was abundant with wildlife, now more precious than ever, because much of it is endangered by a society that does not understand or appreciate living creatures and their helpful, peaceful way of life. Cedar and pine trees that kept their green cloak the year round always impressed me as a child. I also loved the many fences so necessary to a farm.

"In my quilt, I have tried to depict a peaceful scene—a farmhouse beside a pine tree, green grass, birds, a cottontail rabbit, and the sun, without which a farm could not exist."

This design does evokes a sense of peace and serenity, partially through the subject matter but also through the low-keyed colors Mrs. Niebauer used to carry through the design (see page 11). The three-dimensional rabbit ears and rabbit tail add a touch of whimsey. This mostly patchwork design is complicated to construct, because there are so many different pieces.

Each finished block measures 12" (30.5cm) square.

One block takes the following:

One of each piece with the following exceptions:

13—2 doors and windows
F—2 fence rails
G—2 fence posts
I—2 ears

The birds are made with the outline (stem) stitch. The door and window are appliquéd in place to the house with a blanket stitch. The doorknob is a French knot, and the peephole and the windowpanes in the door are made with the stem stitch. To make the rabbit, pad the body lightly as you sew it in place. Make the ears separately and tuck the ends under the head. Form a cotton ball about ½" (1.3cm) in diameter and blind stitch it in place to make the tail. The whiskers are long satin stitches.

70

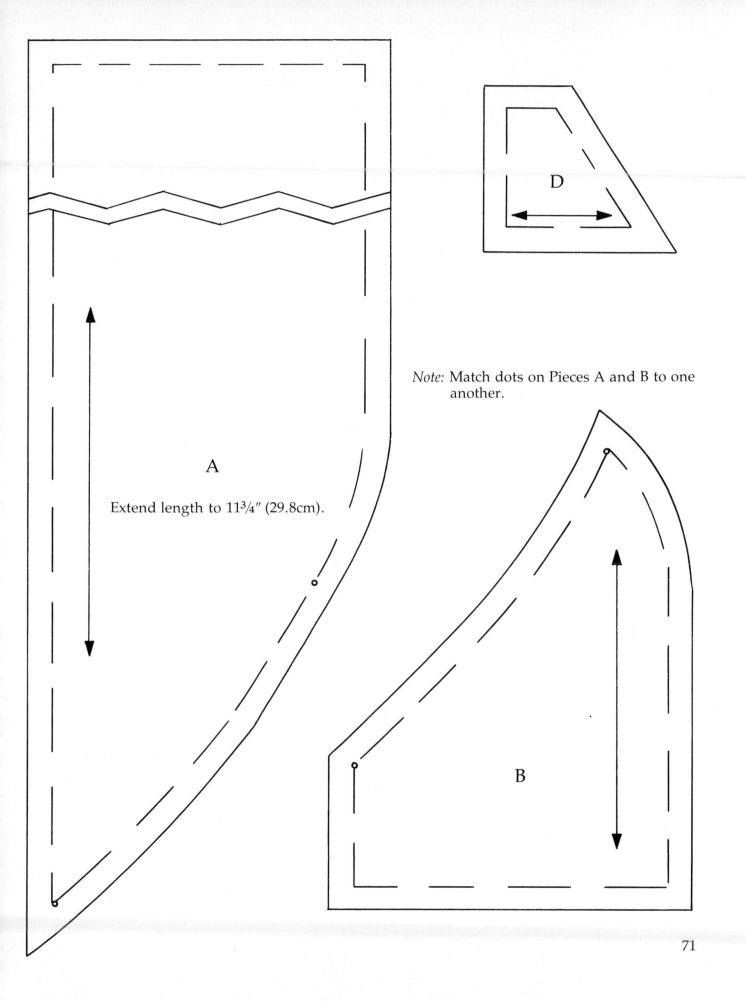

D

*Note:* Match dots on Pieces A and B to one another.

A

Extend length to 11¾″ (29.8cm).

B

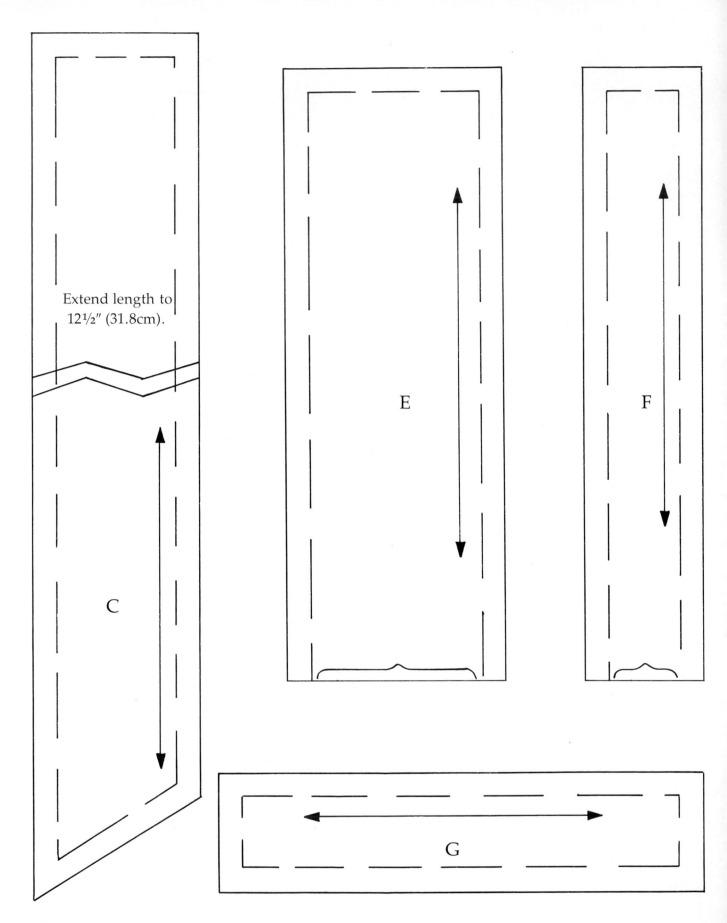

Extend length to
12½" (31.8cm).

C

E

F

G

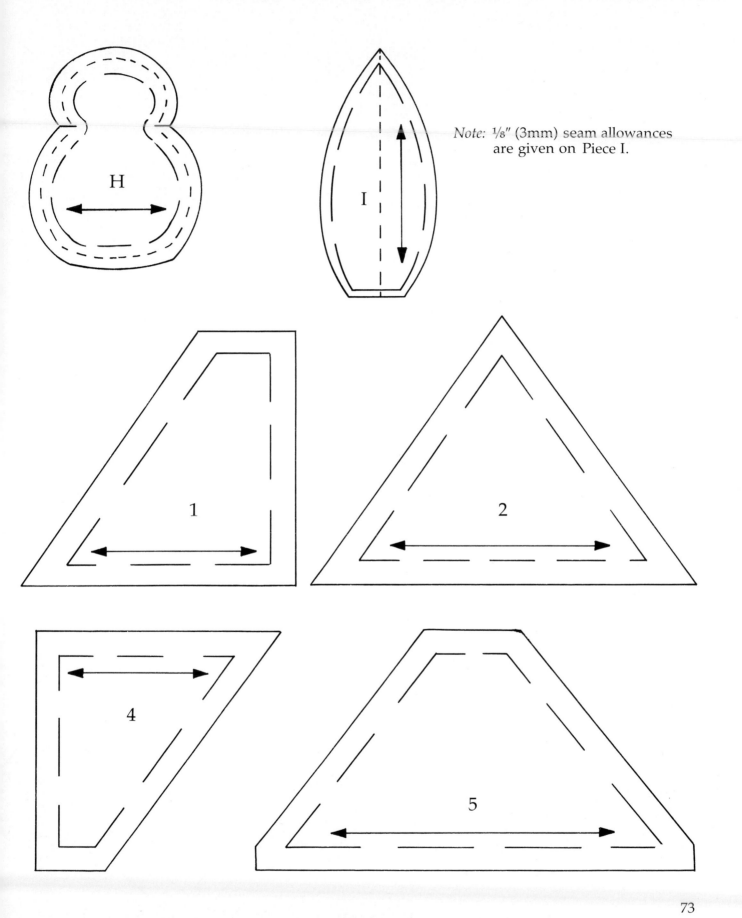

Note: ⅛″ (3mm) seam allowances are given on Piece I.

H

I

1

2

4

5

73

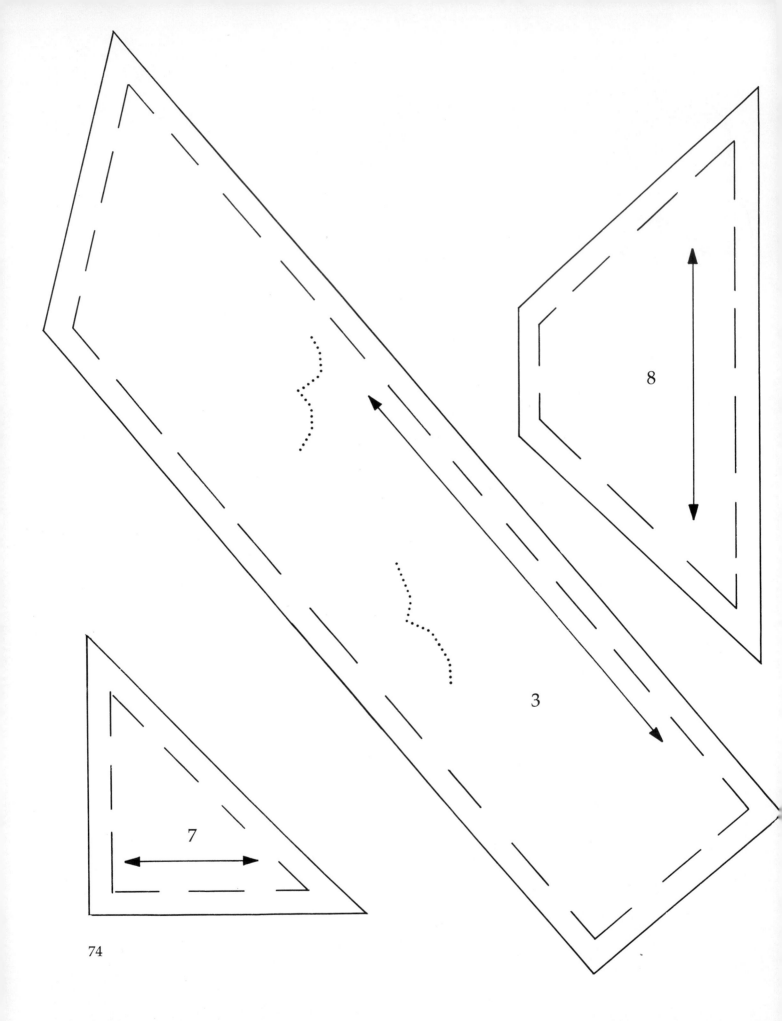

74

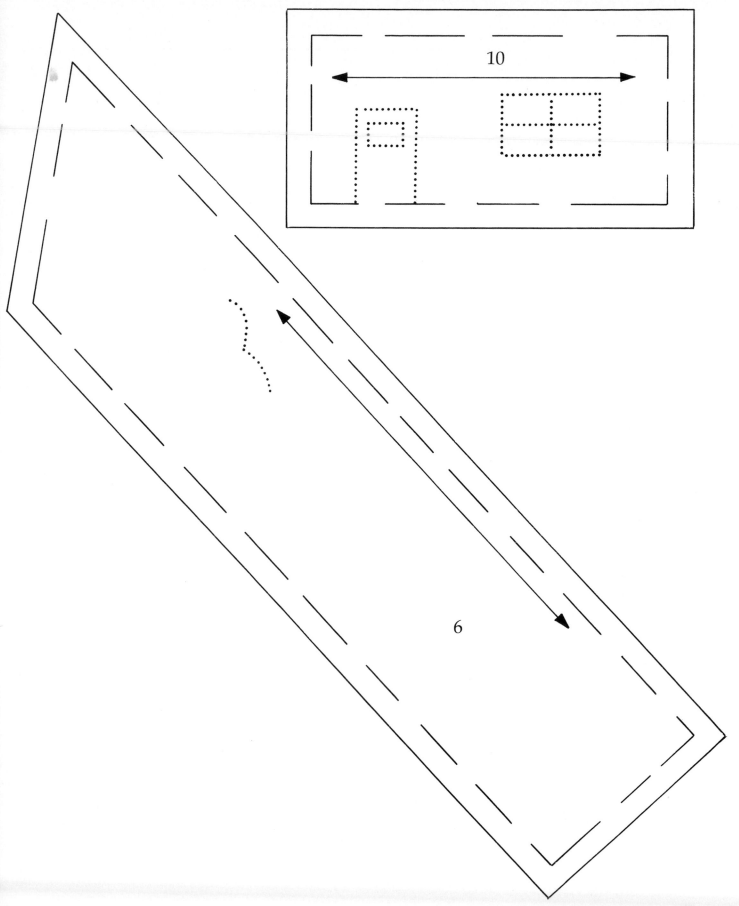

10

6

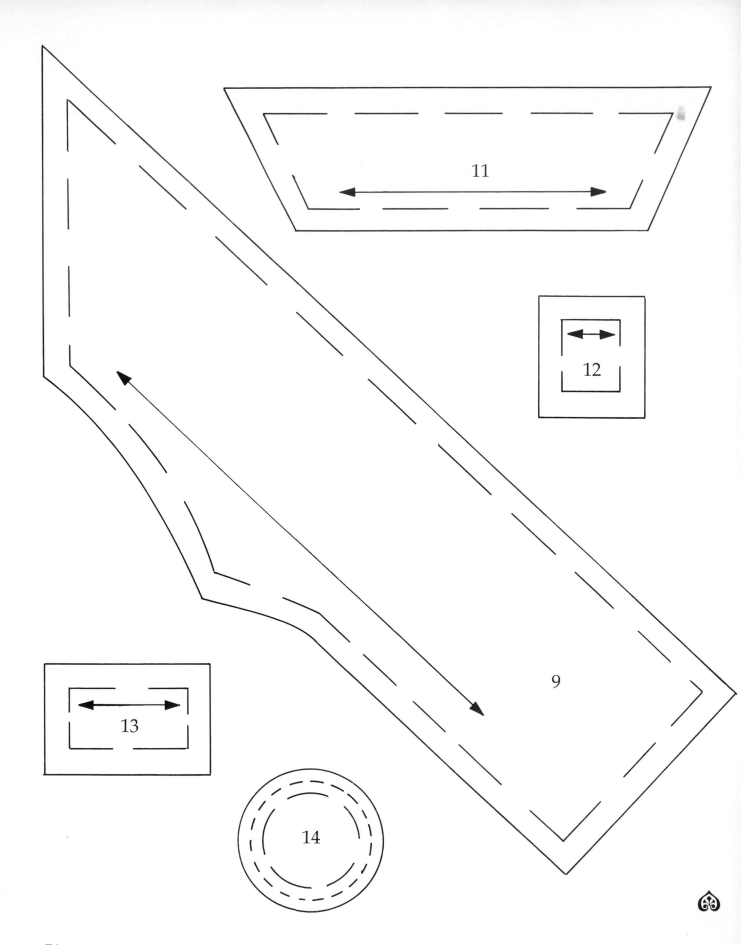

11

12

13

9

14

# USA*

Mrs. Velma H. Culbert
Beggs, Oklahoma

"The official American Bicentennial emblem helped inspire the design of this *USA* quilt pattern. The A's forming the points of the star are continuously united, symbolic of the meaning of the United States of America. It is an appliqué design and can be used as a one pattern quilt or will harmonize nicely with other patterns. The red, white, and blue of the flag of the United States of America seem to be a perfect color choice."

This Bicentennial quilt design has timeless appeal in its simplicity and folk art style. It took a Judges' Choice award in the *Progressive Farmer* quilt contest. We think it would be spectacular set into the back of a denim jacket.

Each finished block measures 14½" (36.8cm) square.

One block takes the following:
5 U's
5 S's
5 A's
Background square—15" x 15"
  (38.1cm x 38.1cm)

The best way to put this design together is to first sew the A's together at each leg to form the center star. Then turn the edges under and appliqué the star to the center of the background square. Note that the center triangle of the A has ⅛" (3mm) seam allowances.

Use the star as a positioning point for the S's, then the U's.

---

*Judges' Choice

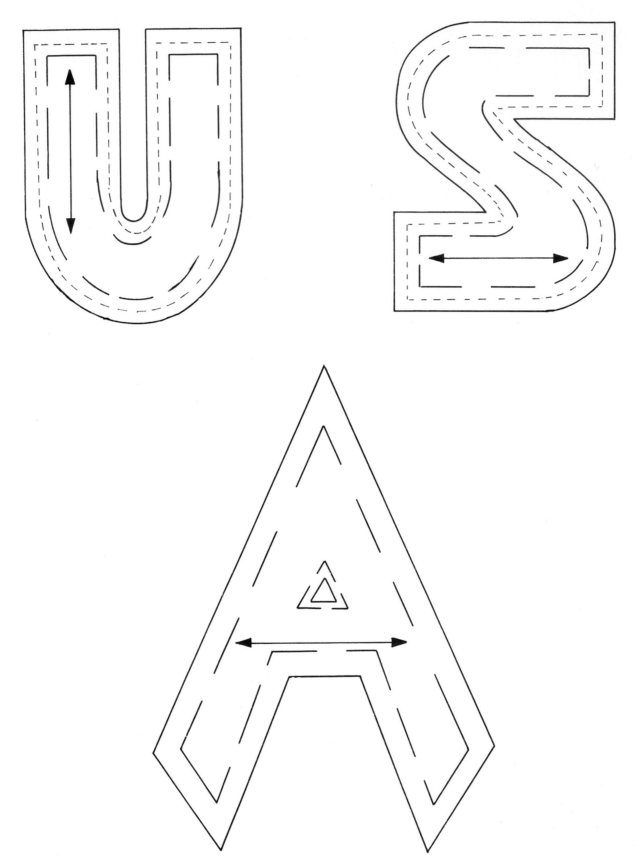

# WHEEL
Mrs. Cleo Kelly
Bardwell, Kentucky

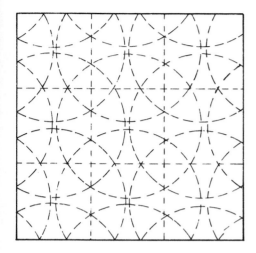

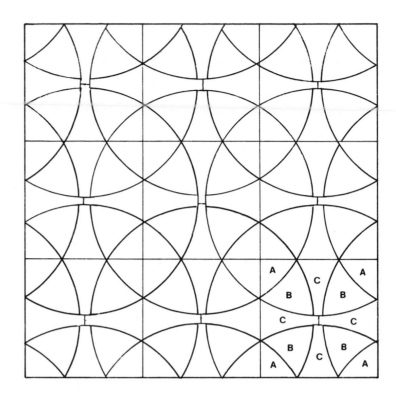

"I was born and reared on a farm and lived there for 45 years. I have many precious memories from the time I spent there. In thinking back, I particularly remember the farm implements that were used to plant, cultivate, and harvest our crops each year. Then I thought of all the new equipment that farmers have today: combines, huge tractors, and much other sophisticated machinery. My mind centered around wheels—all the many wheels on a farm.

"Back in my time, we used binders to cut wheat, mowers to cut hay, hay rakes to rake up the hay in rows so we could pitch the hay onto the old two-horse wagon with the hay frame on it. We also used cultivators to plow our corn. I remember, too, that we had a two-horse surrey with fringe around the top, and, of course, a one-horse buggy. We also had the old red wheel-operated grist mill that we used to grind up corn for chicken feed."

Mrs. Kelly's fascinating patchwork pattern is made up of a small block repeated 9 times to form one large quilt block. The color placement is carefully worked out to give the over-lapping circles so reminiscent of geometric doodles. (This design also looks like a shamrock, especially when the triangles are green.)

Each small block measures 7" (17.8cm) square.

One block takes the following:

A—4 corner sections
B—4 curved triangles
C—4 center sections

Notice that Mrs. Kelly used three different color combinations in her design. You must work out your color scheme in advance to know how many squares of each color combination you will need.

To construct the design, sew the A's to the B's, then sew the AB sections to the C pieces, matching the dot on A to the dot on C, and aligning the lower edges. Then sew C's together in the center, folding the extensions out of the way where they are not needed.

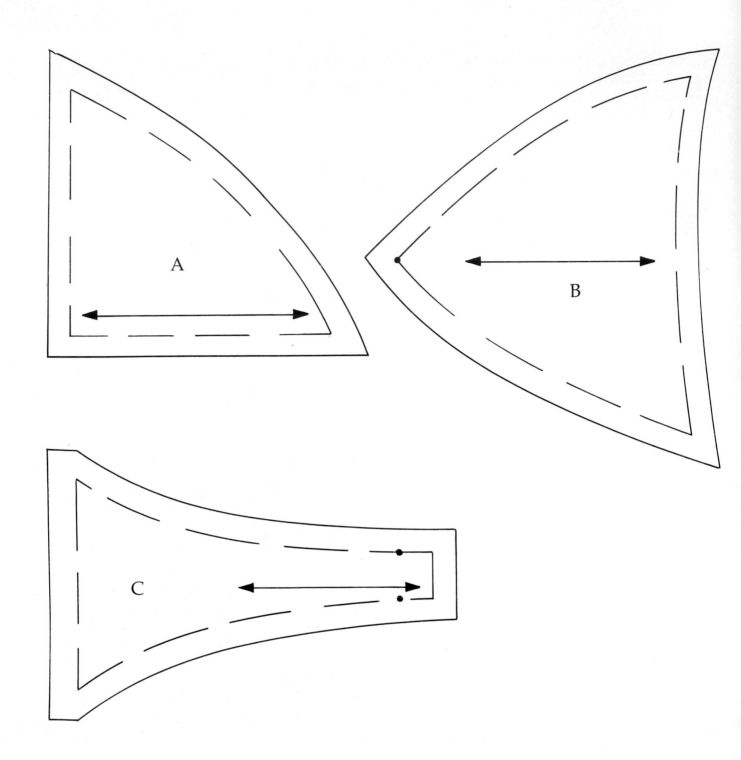